REVELATION &
REVOLUTION IN ISLAM

REVELATION & REVOLUTION IN ISLAM

Ziaul Haque

ATLANTIC PUBLISHERS & DISTRIBUTORS

Distributed by
ATLANTIC PUBLISHERS AND DISTRIBUTORS
B-2, Vishal Enclave, New Delhi-110 027
Phones 5413460, 5429987

Sales Office
4346/4C, Ansari Road, Darya Ganj,
New Delhi-110 002
Phones 3273880, 3285873
Fax 91-11-3285873

Typeset at
APD Computer Graphics, Delhi
Printed at
Tarun Offset Printers, Delhi-110 053

CONTENTS

Chapter 1	Introduction.	1
Chapter 2	The Quranic Concepts of Revelation and Revolution.	8
Chapter 3	The Social Mission of Prophet–Revolutionaries.	30
Chapter 4	The Prophet–Revolutionaries & the Proletariat.	44
Chapter 5	The Concepts of Jihad, Hijra & Social Equality.	53
Chapter 6	What is Truth?	71
Chapter 7	Adam–The First Prophet who Fought Against Ignorance and Evil.	97
Chapter 8	Nuh–The Prophet who Led the Poor.	111
Chapter 9	Hud–The Prophet who Defied the Arrogant.	119

Chapter 10	Salih and his Fight for Social Equality.	125
Chapter 11	Ibrahim–The Prophet who Proclaimed Truth and Justice.	133
Chapter 12	Yousuf: The Prophet who Persevered in Adversity.	150
Chapter 13	Shu'ayb and his Struggle Against Economic Injustice.	159
Chapter 14	Musa–The Prophet who Liberated the Slaves.	166
Chapter 15	'Isa–The Prophet who Led the Weak.	174
Chapter 16	Muhammad–The Last Prophet –Revolutionary.	189
Chapter 17	Two Moralities: Revolutionary and Feudalist–Capitalist.	217
Chapter 18	Prophets and Revolutionaries.	234
Chapter 19	Conclusion.	251
INDEX		257

1

INTRODUCTION

Eversince human beings originated on this earth and human communities, societies, civilizations appeared, and human thought, perception, emotion and intellect evolved, the brute forces of evil and ignorance, oppression and falsehood have been opposing the forces of goodness, justice, light and truth. These contradictory forces took the concrete forms of groups, tribes, and classes who had antagonistic interests and purposes of their existence. One class or group, after acquiring power and control of the basic means of production (land, water, mines etc), tried to subdue and enslave the other classes.

In this eternal conflict the more powerful groups and classes lived and survived by oppressing or killing the weak ones in an inferno of discord and disharmony. In this class struggle and war every one desperately ran to acquire power—physical, material, economic, political and intellectual. And power flowed from accumulations of wealth, material goods, possessions and lands, or from the command of labour-force or armies of followers. The god-kings, pharaohs, oppressors and slave-owners of pre-capitalist ancient societies relied on naked force, material possessions and man-power.

Revelation and Revolution, as the title and the subtitle of this book show, discusses the lives, missions,

characters, roles, struggles and achievements of the prophet-revolutionaries who appeared in the pre-capitalist ancient times to liberate the suffering humanity from the heavy yoke of oppression and slavery. In their struggles against the forces of evil and oppression, the prophet-revolutionaries combined the roles of prophets and revolutionaries within the religious framework. This book therefore focuses on the nature of prophecy, revelation and revolution. What was divinely revealed to a prophet-revolutionary was truth which he conveyed to his contemporaries in the religious medium.

But what is truth? What is the social significance of the religious conception of revelatory truth, what is the difference between a revelatory truth, a revolutionary principle and a rigid ritual or cult which, after sometime when any revolution decays and ossifies, is attributed to the early pristine principles?

These and other related questions about revelation and revolution will be raised and answered in this book in order to clarify the basic differences between a divinely-inspired prophet of ancient times and a modern revolutionary who struggles in a (feudal) capitalist formation to emancipate the oppressed working classes.

The religious scriptures, the Qur'an and the Bible employ allegories, metaphors, similes and parables from nature and human life in order to explain the social and economic problems of the pre-feudal pastoral and tribal societies. But they do not clearly reveal the exact economic characters or roles of various classes fighting against each other for the control of the basic means of production and sources of power and control. The broad appellations and general categories of 'oppressors' and 'exploiters', (*Zalimun*) 'rich' and 'powerful (*al-mutrafun*), 'arrogant' and 'insolent' (*al-mustakbarun*), 'lords' and

'chiefs' (*al-mala'a*), god-kings (*fara'ina*, singular *fir'awn*, pharaoh), on the one side; and the 'oppressed' and 'exploited' (*al-mustad'afun*), 'poor' and weak, humble and 'lowly' (*al-ardhalun*), on the other, generally characterize the 'class composition' of the pre-feudal ancient communities in which the prophet-revolutionaries led the poor proletariat and struggled against the oppressors —slave-owners, merchants, lords and priests etc.

There were many prophet-revolutionaries, so says the Qur'an, who appeared in different communities throughout the ages of whom, some are mentioned in the Qur'an and others are not. The Qur'an generally deals with those prophets who were close to the Arab tradition; that is, who appeared in or around the vast Arab Peninsula (Qur'an, 40: 78; 4: 163–165). The common and chief trait of these prophet-revolutionaries is that they revolted and fought against the communities of oppressors, *Qura Zalima,* and guided, mobilized and organized the rebels, the poor and the weak who believed in truth, sincerity, social equality, brotherhood and justice and aspired to establish a just and egalitarian social order in place of an iniquitous social order.

The prophet-revolutionaries, Nuh, Hud, Salih, Ibrahim, Shu'ayb, Musa, 'Isa, Muhammad and others were all initially rejected by the people in general and were branded as madmen, sorcerers, soothsayers, poets, idealists, liars, and agents of foreigners because they destabilized their communities, threatened the established social orders of evil and corruption, and, gave new standards, criteria, and values of truth, social equality, justice and brotherhood, humility and selflessness, in place of falsehood, oppression, iniquity, exploitation, greed, pride, lust and selfishness which were ingrained in the people who rejected them.

The prophet-revolutionaries and their followers, as dedicated men, sacrificed everything for the cause of truth and social equality: their lives, their hearths and homes, wealth and possessions, families and tribes, comforts and personal advantages. They migrated to places of safety and security from where they waged ceaseless wars against the old order to transform it into a new order of justice and equality, a paradise of truth, love and brotherhood on earth. In the words of the Qu'ran, theirs was a bargain in which "God hath purchased of the believers (in truth and equality) their persons and their goods; for theirs (in return) is the Garden of Paradise. They fight in His cause, and slay and are slain; a promise binding on Him in Truth, through Torah, Evangel and the Qur'an. And who is more faithful to his covenant than God? Then rejoice in the bargain which ye (O Muslim revolutionaries!) have concluded. That is the supreme achievement." (9 : 111).

A prophet-revolutionary combines two roles: the role of a prophet who is divinely-inspired and guided by the divine truth; and the role of a revolutionary or a rebel who brings radical changes in the old social order and transforms modes and patterns of human behaviour, thought, emotions and morals according to the revelatory truth. Thus revelation is revolution and revolution is revelation. The revelation, at the first stage revivifies or transforms the prophet-revolutionary, and afterwards, this revelatory truth morally and socially resurrects the corrupt and 'dead' society like the rain which brings life to a dead and barren land.

The prophet-revolutionaries were human beings. (13: 38; 14: 10–11). They were divinely-inspired and were charged with the heavy responsibility of proclaiming truth (33: 7–8). They lived and worked, struggled and fought in a pre-feudal and pre-scientific society or age where religion was the main language, idiom and mode for perceiving and expressing reality. Religion was the vehicle and framework through which their messages, ideas, conceptions, words, and struggles were expressed. Everything was cast and impressed in the mould of religion. It was the age of religious mentality. And every emotion, thought, idea and imagination were tied to theology.

Now we live under revolutionary times. This is the age of the ordinary, working masses and of science, industry, reason nd rationalism. The scientific method employed in the natural, social and biological sciences for discovering new knowledge and truth, has replaced the religious method of perceiving reality. The modern class struggle is waged by modern revolutionaries. They are the vanguard of the struggle of the proletariat. They are not prophets. The social aims of the ancient prophets and modern revolutionaries, more or less, are the same: the emancipation of the oppressed. But the methods of liberation always changed as the social and economic formations and modes of perceiving and conceiving social reality changed, from pastoral tribal to feudal and capitalist.

This book is a modest attempt to show what the Qur'an says about prophet-revolutionaries, their times, their social missions and their struggles against god-kings, slave-owners, usurer-merchants, high priests, lords and chiefs, the oppressors who had throughout the ages enslaved the poor and weak masses and classes. Our chief source is the Qur'an. The Qur'an is not only an objective record of the origin, and development of Muhammad's social mission as a prophet-revolutionary, but it is also a cogent exposition and narration of the lives, struggles and careers of the great prophets who preceded him, like Ibrahim, Musa, and 'Isa.

The book is divided into three parts. The first part (Revelation and Revolution) consists of six chapters which deal with the Quranic concepts of revelation, revolution, social mission of the prophet-revolutionaries, the nature of the proletariat emancipated by them, the social significance of the concepts of *Hijra* (migration), *Jihad* (war), justice and social equality and the nature of truth divinely revealed to the prophet-revolutionaries.

Part two of the book (Prophet-revolutionaries in the Qur'an) comprising ten chapters, discusses in detail the lives and missions of ten important prophet-revolutionaries. The third part (Prophecy, Revolution and Morality) analyses the ideas of prophecy, modern revolution and liberation theology. The difference between the revolutionary and feudalist-capitalist moralities is discussed in a separate chapter. The last chapter concludes the discussion.

Some of the chapters of this book have appeared in *Viewpoint* (Lahore) and *Dawn* (Karachi) in brief outlines. These have been further elaborated and enlarged. New chapters have been added to make the book coherent and consistent. The author expresses his gratitude to the editors and publishers of *Viewpoint* and *Dawn* for granting their permission to do so.

For the English translations of the Quranic verses quoted in this book the monumental work of 'Abdullah Yusuf Ali: *The Holy Qur'an : Text, Translation and Commentary*, (Lahore: Sheikh Muhammad Ashraf, 1934), has been used with some modifications and additions of the author's own interpretations.

I must thank Sayyid Ghulam Murtaza Shah, the

Librarian of Masum Shah Library, Sukkur, Sind, and his assistants, Gul Muhammad, Mushtaq Ali, and Dhani Bakhsh for their help and cooperation in utilizing the modest and meagre resources of the library. This library is a very small island in a vast ocean of illiteracy and poverty in this upper part of the Indus valley. This region is one of the most underdeveloped areas of Pakistan. Mr. Najam Sethi of Vanguard Books Ltd., Lahore, also deserves my thanks for discreetly publishing the book.

SUKKUR, SIND ZIAUL HAQUE
February, 1987.

* In the reference of Quranic chapters and verses in the parentheses, , the first number refers to the *Sura* or chapter; and the second number to the verse actually quoted, thus in (2 : 164), number 2 refers to the second Sura of Baqara, and the second number to the verse number 164 of this sura.

2

THE QURANIC CONCEPTS OF REVELATION AND REVOLUTION.

The Qur'an,* literally a 'reading', is a Book of guidance to those "who are righteous, who believe in the Unseen, are steadfast in prayer (i.e. higher values of truth, equality, justice, sincerity etc), and spend out of what We have given to them; and who believe in the Revelation to thee (O Muhammad!). . (2: 1–4).

Revelation is something revealed, manifested, disclosed or made known. It is an enlightenment, an evidence of reality and a confirmation of truth. It is a clear sign, a proof or indication, meaning or signification for a seer which calls for observation, reflection and understanding. Every divinely inspired new idea, suggestion, thought, scientific invention, equalitarian social order, discovery of truth is a revelation because it adds to human knowledge, guidance and welfare and liberates the shackled minds, morals and emotions and emancipates oppressed human beings from the forces of evil, tyranny and superstition.

The universe, the earth, the heavens, the sun and the moon, day and night, light and darkness, change of sea-

---

* Consisting of 114 *Suras* (Chapters), Meccan and Medinan, the Qur'an was revealed to prophet Muhammad (A.D. 570–632), during a period of twenty–three years (*Circa* 610–632) in a tribal and pre-feudal society of the Hijaz (Arabia).

sons, are all revelations and signs for those who are alive, have wisdom and insight: who have eyes to see, ears to hear, hearts to feel and minds to reflect and understand.

The natural, social and historical phenomena, in all their manifestations, mysteries and wonders, are all revelations, signs and evidence of truth for those who can explore, investigate, discover the truth and understand it.

1. Signs, Symbols and Metaphors:

Divine inspirations, Divine scriptures revealed to the prophets, prophets' missions for emancipating the oppressed and the down-trodden of their contemporary societies, their words and deeds, their ideas and ideals, their lives and characters, their struggles and strifes for the proclamation of truth, are all signs.

All these God's signs by which He calls us to think, feel and reflect, are everywhere, in our selves, in our very inner consciences, in our hearts and minds, in the starry nights, in the deep oceans, and in the vast space, in our souls, in our intellectual, rational, emotional and moral faculties, in nature, is human society, and in history, so says the Qur'an, the holy Book revealed to Muhammad (Son of 'Abd Allah), the last prophet-revolutionary, who was an inspired man of God and truth.

Every stream, river, cloud, wind, or rain which brings life to a 'dead' land is a revelation; and every social revolution which resurrects a 'dead' community is a revelation. "Behold", says the Qur'an,

> " in the creation of the heavens and the earth; in the alternation of the night and the day; in the sailing of the ships through the ocean for the profit of mankind; in the rain which God sends down from

> the skies; and the life which He gives therewith to an earth that is dead; in the beasts of all kinds that He scatters through the earth; in the change of the winds, and the clouds which they trail like their slaves between the sky and the earth;–here indeed are signs, *ayat,* for a people that are wise" (2: 164).

For the Qur'an, the very birth of man, his society, cultures, civilizations, languages, races, tribes and clans and the rise and fall of nations are all signs which the people must ponder and take admonition from them:

> "Among His signs is this that He created you from dust; and then,–behold, ye are men scattered (far and wide). And among His Signs is this, that he created for you mates from among yourselves, that ye may dwell in tranquillity with them, and He has put love and mercy between your (hearts); verily in that are signs for those who reflect. And among His signs is the creation of the heavens and the earth, and the variations in your languages and your colours: verily in that are signs for those who know. And among His signs is the sleep that ye take by night and by day and the quest that ye (make for livelihood) out of His bounty: verily in that are signs for those who hearken. And among His signs He shows you the lightning by way both of fear and of hope, and He sends down rain from the sky and with it gives life to the earth after it is dead: verily in that are signs for those who are wise. And among His signs is this that heavens and earth stand by His command: then when He calls you, by a single call, from the earth, behold ye are resurrected" (30 : 20–25).

"On the earth are signs for those of assured faith and also in your own selves: will ye not then see?" So affirms the Qur'an. (51: 20–21). Revelation is the light "wherewith God guideth all who seek His good pleasure to ways of peace and safety, and leadeth then out of darkness, by His will, into the light – guideth to a path that is straight". (5: 16).

Thus revelation makes things clear. It dissipates darkness and removes the mist which beclouds minds and hearts. It is like the star of piercing brightness in the dark and gloomy night of sorrow, sin and suffering when things, ideas, relationships, institutions, thoughts, passions, emotions, morals, values, distinctions, marks and signs become murky, muddled and confused. Revelation is the flash of truth. It is like a seed sprouting through the hard crust of the soil, coming from darkness to light; or is it like the gushing of a stream which flows over the tortuous paths and dashes against stones and blocks. It is the word that distinguishes good from evil, true from false and light from dark. It is a criterion of judgement and a standard to judge and measure the worth of a thing:

> "And We sent down the Book (i.e. Revelation) to thee", says the Qur'an to prophet Muhammad, "for the express purpose, that thou shouldst make clear to them those things in which they differ, and that it should be a guide and a mercy to those who believe (in truth). And God sends down rain from the skies, and gives therewith life to the earth after its death: verily in this is a sign for those who listen". (16: 64–65).

Before Muhammad, other prophets also received revelations by which they guided their followers to truth, equality, goodness and brotherhood.

> "We gave Musa (Moses) the Book and followed him up with a succession of Apostles; We gave 'Isa

(Jesus Christ) ibn Maryam clear (Signs) and strengthened him with the holy spirit". (2 : 87).

"Can he who was dead, and to whom We gave life and a light whereby he can walk amongst men, be like him who is in the depths of darkness, from which he can never come out? Thus to those who reject (Truth) their own deeds seem pleasing". (6 : 122).

The Qur'an uses the simile of winds laden heavily with rain which bring life to a dead land. So are resurrected the 'dead' who lose their moral vigour, inner purity and social stability and vitality due to numerous evils, weaknesses and disabilities of oppression, injustice, jealousy, arrogance, ignorance and superstition; the biting frost of iniquity and the blighting exploitation of man by man, destroy the social fabric:

"It is He who sendeth the winds like heralds of glad tidings, going before His Mercy: when they have carried the heavy – laden clouds, We drive them to a land that is dead, make rain to descend thereon, and produce every kind of harvest therewith: thus shall We raise up the dead: perchance ye may remember. From the land that is clean and good, by the Will of its Cherisher, springs up produce (rich) after its kind. But from the land that is bad, springs up nothing but that is niggardly. Thus do We explain the signs by various (symbols) to those who are grateful". (7 : 57–58).

A just and equalitarian social order is like a good and fertile land, prosperous, healthy, balanced and progressive which develops abilities, powers and talents of its members to the full potential; but an unjust and iniquitous social order riven with corruption and evil, discord and disunity, jealousy and fraud, is like a bad land where nothing, or only niggardly, grows.

According to the Qur'an, this description or elucidation of resurrecting a 'dead' land or a 'dead' people is symbolical and metaphorical only to explain the revolutionary and life-giving role of revelation in radically restructuring the 'dead', obsolete, decadent and lifeless social and economic institutions and relations of a society.

A social revolution has also a revelationary role; it descends into the hearts and minds of the once morally dead people and enthuses life and spirit into them, through a new truth which enlightens and guides the people.

Revelation is the mind and soul whereas revolution is the change and transformation which is wrought into the social body, into the institutions, ideas and emotions as in the modern class struggle between the capitalists and the working classes, science constitutes the mind and revolution is the social change. Both complement each other. Without revelation or scientific theory, any change is a blind jump into the dark, and without its aim of change or revolution, science or revelation is a mere sermon or admonition.

From these Quranic Verses quoted at length, it appears that this religious/theological conception of revelation as truth, light, or knowledge to a divinely inspired prophet, 'strengthened with the holy spirit' is metaphorical and allegorical. This mode of expressing reality in simple and natural terms, in similes and examples, is common to religion, poetry and folk literature of beduins and peasants from ancient times. It is to be understood symbolically. A metaphor is a resemblance and illustration of the actual and real. It is simplificution of a complex phenomenon incomprehensible to simple folks.

The Qur'an uses similes and parables of mosquitoes, flies, spiders, birds, plants, gardens, rivers and mountains in order to explain the complex and intricate social and economic problems, struggle of goodness against evil. It compares the iniquitous social order of oppressors and exploiters (of the poor and weak) to spider's web, which is inherently weak and unstable and cannot stand in the face of a revolutionary storm: "The parable of those who take protectors other than God is that of the spider, who builds (to itself) a house; bu truly, the flimsiest of houses is the spider's house: —if they but know. . . . . and such are the parables We set for mankind, but only those understand them who have knowledge." (29 : 41).

The religious conception of revelation simply connotes the divine inspiration of a prophet who is a man of God, a righteous, truthful and honest human being and whose innocent heart, pure and clear conscience faithfully reflect the divine light and revelation (2 : 97). Revelations and signs can be understood and appreciated only by those whose hearts and minds, souls and consciences are not stained with the dross of lust and greed, and are not sullied with the taint of pride and arrogance. In the heart of a man of God the stains of selfishness and pride are washed away. He is a humble, honest, simple and courageous human being. His ways are sincere and his life is open.

This metaphorical conception of revelation or divine inspiration of truth was the pre-scientific simple perception to represent the practical method for emancipating the oppressed and weak human beings from the slavery of the powerful oppressors who did not believe in truth, justice, equality and gooness but instead clung to brute force and evil. It was the religious expression of reality in religious terms and in simple parables, similes, metaphors and symbols which the man of the pre-scientific and pre-industrial age could perceive and understand.

2. Social Revolution:

Modern social revolution is total and radical change in the decadent social structures, ideas and thought patterns. It is the scientific perception and vision of a modern man of scientific age, and hence it envisages a scientific method to discover truth in order to liberate the oppressed classes from the bondage of modern semi-feudal and capitalist classes. Modern revolution is therefore a theory as well as a practical method. Prescientific revelation and modern scientific revolution are thus two different perceptions of social reality and two different methods to understand and change it. One method is pre-scientific, religious and theological in conception which traces every effect and event to a Divine plan; the other is scientific and socio-economic which explains changes and revolutions, class-struggles and transformations according to certain historical, natural or dialectical laws. Both these methods, revelation of a prophet, and radical change of a decadent social order by modern revolutionaries under certain scientific, natural and historical laws, are not different in essence; both are the methods to discover new truth and new criterion and therewith to bring equilibrium, justice, equality and harmony to the iniquitous and chaotic social order and thus liberate the oppressed classes. This entails the establishment of a new social order according to the new truth and new criterion, which is free from evil, corruption, tyranny and exploitation.

The prophet-revolutionaries also brought radical

changes in their contemporary societies, in morals, emotions, thought-patterns, social behaviour and manners. But the methods of modern revolutionaries and the prophet-revolutionaries are different in one aspect: one is scientific the other is pre-scientific and religious. The former is essentially linked to modern science and the latter is tied to theology i.e. the conception that social and historical changes can only be explained and understood as Divine plan or theodicy. The Qur'an describes this theological perception of revelation in the following beautiful verses:

> "By the star when it goes down, your companion (i.e. Muhammad) is neither astray nor being misled nor does he say aught of (his own) desire. It is no less than inspiration sent down to him: he was taught by one Mighty in power endued with wisdom; for he appeared (in stately form) while he was in the highest part of the horizon. Then he approached and came closer, and was at a distance of but two bow-lengths or (even) nearer; so did God convey the inspiration (*awha*) to His servant – (conveyed) what He (meant) to convey. The (Prophet's mind and) heart in no way falsified that which he saw. Will ye then dispute with him concerning what he saw? For indeed he saw him at a second descent, near the sidra (lote) tree beyond which none may pass: near it is the garden of Abode. Behold! the sidra tree was shrouded (in mystery unspeakable); his sight never swerved nor did it go wrong for truly did he see, of the signs of his Lord, the Greatest." (53: 1–18).

Revelation is the truth which confirms other revealed truths which preceded it in various communities and epochs. "That which We have revealed to thee of the

Book is the truth,—confirming what was (revealed) before it: for God is assuredly—with respect to His servants—Well acquainted and Fully observant. Then We have given the Book for inheritance to such of Our servants as We have chosen. . . ." (35: 31–32).

3. The Divine Source:

All the revelations which came to different prophets in different societies emanated from a single divine or (supra) natural source of wisdom, knowledge and power. The Qur'an was revealed to prophet Muhammad during a long period of almost twenty-three years, from A.D. 610 to 632. It is a revelation which confirms the previous revelations and testifies to the struggle of the prophet-revolutionaries against the forces of evil and oppression, darkness and iniquity.

Societies change and so change their over-all social orders, systems and structures throughout the ages. The prophet-revolutionaries lived in different social orders and formations: pastoral, tribal, nomadic, pre-feudal and feudal, but the basic nature of truth revealed in their teachings, messages, lives and characters was the same. The missions and struggles of the prophets had common aims: emancipation of the oppressed and weak, and proclamation of truth, and establishment of a social order based on the principles of social equality, justice and brotherhood. "And We sent to them an apostle from among themselves, (saying)' Obey God! Ye have no other god but Him. Will ye not fear Him" (23:32). The values of truth, social equality, justice, brotherhood, goodness and sincerity flow from the conception of Divine Unity. The oppressors and exploiters of the poor also rejected the message of truth and social equality; but this did not make any difference for the struggles of the prophets. Truth triumphed over falsehood, and social equality defeated the forces of oppression and tyranny. The rich rejected the truth and refused to cease their tyranny of the oppressed:

> "And the chiefs of his (apostle's) people, who disbelieved and denied the meeting in the Hereafter, and to whom We had given wealth and comforts of this life, said: He is no more than a man like yourselves; he eats of that of which ye eat, and drinks of what ye drink. If ye obey a man like yourselves, behold it is certain ye will be lost." (23: 33–34).

The oppressors refuse to recognize the truth brought by the prophets and instead conspire and plot to tempt the men of God to compromise with their social order of evil and oppression:

> "Or do they not recognize their apostle, that they deny him? Or do they say: He is possessed? Nay, he has brought them the truth, but most of them hate the truth. If the truth had followed their lusts and desires, truly the heavens and the earth and all beings therein would have been corrupted . . ." (23: 69–71).

The revelation and truth brought by a prophet is therefore the light which guides the people, shows them the right path and gives them the criterion with which to distinguish right from wrong and true from false. This divine inspiration comes to his heart and mind in the form of an idea, thought or suggestion which is then expressed and explained in human language, social idioms, words and sentences and which his contemporary human beings understand. Truth discovered is conveyed and communicated to the people in their own language.

Parables, similes, examples and metaphors from nature

and human life are meant to convey the inner sense and meaning of this inspiration. The Quranic parables and metaphors, as we discuss them in a separate section, are intended to explain and simplify complex social problems to the simple people:

> "It is not fitting for a man", says the Qur'an to prophet Muhammad, "that God should speak to him except by inspiration or from behind a veil, or by the sending of a messenger to reveal, with God's permission, what God wills: for He is Most High, Most Wise. And thus have We, by Our command, sent inspiration to thee; thou knewest not (before) what was revelation (*Kitab*) and what was faith; but We have made it (Qur'an) a light wherewith We guide such of our servants as We will; and verily thou dost guide (men) to the straight path, the way of God to whom belongs whatever is in the heavens and whatever is on earth. Behold (how) all affairs tend towards God." (42: 51–52).

4. The Central Idea of Revelation:

The central idea of the religious/theological conception of revelation is that God is the source of all power, knowledge, wisdom, goodness, justice and mercy. Actually, He guides, instructs and teaches the prophets in several open and mysterious ways. His wisdom and knowledge are unfathomable and inexhaustible. The wisdom and knowledge, power and goodness bestowed on a prophet, emanate from the Divine source because He alone creates, plans and directs all human and natural affairs as He wishes. Nobody can question Him and scrutinize His plans:

"Say (O prophet!) if the ocean were ink (where-

> with to write out) the words of my Lord, sooner would the ocean be exhausted than would the words of my Lord, even if we added another ocean like it, for its aid. Say: I am but a man like yourselves (but) the inspiration has come to me, that your God is One God: whoever expects to meet his Lord, let him work righteousness, and in the worship of his Lord, admit no one as partner". (18: 109–110).

The inspiration and the discovery of truth is that God is One and only those shall meet Him who do good deeds and admit no one as His equal or partner with Him. Translated into social language this means that the prophet-revolutionary is a courageous man of God. He is a free person and complete surrender to God and higher values (of truth etc.) free him from the bondage of this world. He does not fear any human being who oppresses and exploits other weaker human beings. He stands upright, speaks his truth and declares war against all tyrants and oppressors, against evil, superstition and darkness. He struggles to establish truth, love, equality and justice in society.

He trusts his God and is dedicated to his higher ideals, principles and values of truth, social equality and brotherhood. He rejects the corrupt social system based on iniquity, oppression and persecution of the weak and poor. He is a model of the new values and practises them in his ordinary life. He shuns disharmony in words and deeds. What he says he acts upon. He does not compromise with evil. This is his strength. He breaks all idols of pride, lust, arrogance, insolence, superstition, falsehood, jealousy, selfishness and all false values and false 'gods'.

The prophet is a human being who lives among the

ordinary and common people. He has a family, children and relatives. He lives in a a given society. He suffers like other poor and weak human beings. He is a model of righteous behaviour for others. He teaches and shows by his example how to behave in adversity and prosperity. He practises self-control. He is patient and constant in troubles and tribulations, afflictions and suffering. He is wise, brave, sagacious, tolerant, humble and self-effacing. He is not self-centred but cares and thinks about others. He does not amass riches and other material possessions because he loves higher values of life: simplicity, honesty, knowledge, wisdom, equality, truth, justice, brotherhood and goodness. He does not possess lands, factories, wealth, treasures of gold and silver, slaves and servants:

> "And they say: 'What sort of an apostle is this, who eats food and walks through the streets? Why has not an angel been sent down to him to give admonition with him? Or (why) has not a treasure been bestowed on him, or why has he (not) a garden from which he could eat? The oppressors say: 'Ye follow none other than a man bewitched (mad)'. See what kind of examples they make for thee! But they have gone astray, and never a way will they be able to find. Blessed is He who if that were His will, could give thee wealth better than those – gardens beneath which rivers flow; and He could give thee palaces (secure to dwell in). Nay, they deny the Hour (of Judgement), but We have prepared a Blazing Fire for such as deny the Hour" (25: 7–11).

The prophets were forbearing for the stupidity, ignorance, pettiness and excesses of the ordinary run of people. And for every age and people there was a revealed writing, Book of guidance, wisdom and knowledge which emanated from the Mother of Book, the source and fountainhead or root of all knowledge and wisdom. Therefore, according to the Qur'an, every age has its specific knowledge which supersedes the previous knowledge.

> "We did send apostles before thee (O Muhammad!) and appointed for them wives and children and it was never the part of an apostle to bring a sign except as God permitted (or commanded). For each period is a Book (revealed). God doth remove off or confirm what He pleaseth; with Him is the Mother (or source) of the Book" (13: 38–39).

Commenting on the verse 2 of *Sura* 62; 'Abd Allah Yusuf'Ali' says: God is full sovereign, and therefore cares for all His subjects, including the meanest and most ignorant, and sends His apostles or messengers to them. He is the Holy One, and therefore purifies and sanctifies those who were steeped in superstition and wickedness. He is Extalted in Power, and therefore, He can confer all these blessings on the most unlikely people and no one can stay His hand. He is wise and therefore He instructs in wisdom both through written scriptures and in other ways e.g., by means of a knowledge of life and its laws, and an understanding of His wonderful universe"[1].

5. Just Social Order:

This means that revelation, its truth and light, inspiration and guidance, instruction and scriptures all constitute a method for establishing a just social order of

---

1. "It is He who has sent amongst the unlettered an apostle from among themselves, to rehearse to them His signs, to sanctify them, and to instruct them in scripture, and wisdom,—although they had been, before, in manifest error",– (62 : 2) *The Holy Quran*, III, 1545.

truth and equality. It is a discovery of truth by an inspired and enlightened, wise and honest human being who struggles and strives to guide and purify other people of their weaknesses, sins, evils, shortcomings, and thus leads them to the straight path of truth and salvation.

In the similar way but under changed circumstances of modern times social revolutions under scientific laws and methods change the rigid conditions of people, mobilize their energies and awaken their latent talents. Revolutions purify people of their weaknesses and imperfections, and develop their powers.

Revelation of ancient times and scientific social revolutions of modern times are different ways of perceiving social reality and changing it. As mode of perception, conception, and change of social reality according to Divine inspiration, revelation relates to the pre-scientific epoch when religion was taken to be a sort of primitive science in the sense that what modern science does today in the discovery of truth and knowledge, religion did the same in the pre-industrial society. Truth, knowledge, enlightenment, guidance and liberation of the oppressed human beings were the cherished goals of the Divinely inspired prophets. Modern scientific social revolution aims at the same objectives but under changed circumstances when religious mentality, sensibilities and perception of reality in theological framework have all been replaced by scientific approach and method. The latter sees reality and society as a changing phenomenon since social change is the result of several causes. Religion traced phenomenon only to one cause, the Divine plan. The prophet divines, foresees and connects phenomenon to Divine purpose and plan whereas the modern scientist-revolutionary explains and reasons and connects phenomenon to several causes in the light of modern science.

Science is an improvement upon religion. Religion cannot be said to be inferior to science. Science has replaced religion as an offspring replaces its old and decrepit parents.

Religious revelation and scientific revolution are therefore both expressions of reality and confirmations of truth; but they employ different languages, media, modes and methods to express and realize the truth. The truth and reality of social equality, honesty, justice, brotherhood, love and goodness have always changed. The pastoral society of Moses was different from the settled agricultural society of Jesus Christ, and the pre-feudal mercantile community of Mecca of Muhammad's times.

The prophets, Moses, Jesus Christ and Muhammad were all rebels and revolutionaries who had revolted against the oppression, iniquity, corruption and evil of their respective social orders, nay, social disorders. They fought all their lives for truth, equality, justice and goodness. The purpose of their struggles was to abolish oppression (*Zulm*) in all its forms, says the Qur'an:

"Before thee (O Muhammad!) also the apostles We sent were but men, to whom We granted inspiration: if ye realize this not, ask of those who possess the Message. Nor did We give them bodies that ate no food, nor were they exempt from death. In the end We fulfilled to them Our promise and We saved them and those whom We pleased, but We destroyed those who transgressed beyond bounds. We have revealed for you (O men!) a book in which is a Message for you: will ye not then understand? How many were the populations We utterly destroyed because of their iniquities, setting up in their places other peoples; yet when they felt Our punishment (coming) behold, they (tried to) flee from it. Flee not, but return to the riches and comforts of this life which were given you; and to your homes, in order that ye may be called to account. They used to say: 'Ah: woe to us; we were indeed oppressors (of the weak). And that cry of theirs ceased not, till We made them as a field that is mown, as ashes silent and quenched." (21: 7–15). (See also 11: 100–104).

6. Unjust Social Order:

The Qur'an terms unjust and iniquitous social orders as *Qura Zalima*: the communities of oppressors. The fundamental mission of the prophet-revolutionaries was to destroy them. And their struggle was aimed at abolishing all areas, traces and vestiges of oppression, injustice and tyranny. The prophets were branded by the oppressors as madmen, sorcerers, soothsayers, poets and even agents of foreigners, taught and trained by others because they were determined to overthrow the old order which persecuted the weak and with which the power, wealth and privileges of the oppressors were tied:

> "Those who rejected (truth) said: 'naught is this but a lie which he (the prophet) has forged, and others have helped him at it'. In truth it is they who have put forward an iniquity and a falsehood." (25: 4).
>
> "*Sad*, by the Qur'an, full of admonition (this is the truth). But those who reject (truth) are (steeped) in self-glory, and separatism. How many generations before them did We destroy? In the end they cried (for mercy)–when there was no longer time for being saved! So they wonder that a warner has come to them from among themselves: And the rejecters say: 'This is a sorcerer telling lies'. (38: 1–4).

"Then they turn away from him (the prophet) saying: 'taught (by others), a man possessed:" (44: 14).

Revelation is like day-break, the sun-rising when everything becomes visible, clear and manifest. It is not something which occurs in a vacuum. It underlines the universal and eternal struggle of goodness against evil and oppression. Revelation is directly related to society. The prophets brought radical social and moral changes in their contemporary societies. Its direct concern are the suffering human beings, their freedom, equality, honour and salvation. The purpose of revelation is to guide human beings and make them morally and socially conscious, accountable and responsible:

> "Raised High above ranks (He is) the Lord of the Throne (of anthority) by His command doth He send the spirit (of inspiration) to any of His servants He pleases, that it may warn (men) of the Day of Mutual Meeting" (40:15).

Revelation is the guidance; it is the guidance for the straight path of truth, equality and justice. As mind is to matter, or soul is to body so revelation is to society. It guides society by giving it clarity, criterion of judgement, and norms and standards of enlightenment and right social behaviour and thought-pattern:

> "Say (O Muhammad!) 'Come, I will rehearse what God hath (really) prohibited you from: join not anything as equal with Him (God); be good to your parents, kill not your children on a plea of want;– We provide sustenance for you and for them:– Come not nigh to shameful deeds, whether open or secret; take not life, which God hath made sacred, except by way of justice and law. Thus doth He command you, that ye may learn wisdom. And come not nigh to the orphan's property, except to

improve it, until he attains the age of full strength; give measure and weight with (full) justice:– no burden do We place on any soul, but that which it can bear;–whenever ye speak, speak justly even if a near relative is concerned; and fulfil the covenant of God. Thus doth He command you, that ye may remember. Verily, this is My way leading straight: follow it: follow not (other) paths. They will scatter you about from His (great) path. Thus doth He command you, that ye may be righteous." (6: 151–153).

Revelation teaches human beings to speak the truth, to do justice and to establish social equality. This is the straight path of God. Social laws, economic institutions and customs may change from place to place and from time to time. The principles of truth, equality and justice may take various forms and different institutions for their social expression and actual realization in society. The social, economic and political institutions established by Musa, Ibrahim, Shu'ayb, or Muhammad under Divine inspiration were the means to realize the higher principles of truth, equality and justice. These local or specific institutions related to the social and economic formations in which they lived, worked, thought and struggled against the forces of evil and oppression.

The 'way of life', *din,* of all the Divinely inspired prophets, was the same: the supremacy of truth, equality and justice; but different institutions which were established by the prophets to attain their higher values and principles, always changed. The new social order abrogated the old order as life evolved progressively:

"And We gave Moses the Book (revelation), completing (Our favour) to those who would do right, and explaining all things in detail–and a guide and a mercy, that they might believe in the meeting with their Lord. And this is a Book (revelation) We have revealed as a blessing (to thee O Muhammad!), so follow it and be righteous, that ye may receive mercy. Lest ye should say: 'The Book (revelation) was sent down to two peoples before us, and for our part, we remained unacquainted with all that they learned by assiduous study. (6: 154–156).

"As for those who divide their 'way of life' and break up into sects, thou hast no part in them in the least. Their affair is with God. He will in the end tell them the truth of all that they did. He that doeth good shall have ten times as much to his credit. He that doeth evil shall only be recompensed according to his evil. No wrong shall be done unto (any of) them"

"Say 'verily, my Lord hath guided me to a way that is straight:– a way of life of truth,–the path trod by Ibrahim the true in faith, and he (certainly) joined not gods with God."

"Say: 'Truly, my prayer (devotion) and my service of sacrifice, my life and my death, are (all) for God, the Cherisher of the worlds. No partner hath He: this am I commanded, and I am the first of those who surrender their wills to His Will". (6: 159–163).

Thus, according to the Qur'an, revelation signifies humble submission and surrender of one's entire self, will and power to the higher will, power, plan, wisdom, goodness of a superior Being variously conceived by human mind as the Highest cause, God, or natural/historical force or Energy who reveals itself through various ways, signs, marks, guidelines, social revolutions, inventions, manifestations in nature, in moral and mental faculties of man, his Divine inspirations, intellectual achievements, in history and society. Perceived by limited human minds, deficient faculties, imperfect reasoning processes and limited social circumstances, this overpowering feeling and intense emotion about the presence of a superior, higher and transcendent all-knowing and all-seeing Power is the source of inspiration, enlightenment, truth, wisdom, knowledge and goodness. This is revealed in signs around us and within us. This is revealed in the resurrection of a morally 'dead' person and of 'dead' communities. This process of revelation is a continuous process emanating from an eternal Book which is inexhaustible, whether manifested in the struggles of ancient prophets and modern revolutionaries. Only the times and societies have changed, but the struggle of truth, equality, justice and goodness against the forces of falsehood, iniquity, oppression and evil continues in different colours and garbs, forms and frames. Nature, life and society evolve through contradictions and contrasts.

This discussion of the pre-scientific conception of revelation and the modern conception of scientific social revolution brings us to the important issue of the ends of prophets' social missions and the purpose of Divine inspiration.

3

THE SOCIAL MISSION OF PROPHET–REVOLUTIONARIES

1. The Three Aims of Prophecy:

The *raison d'etre* of Divine revelation and the social mission of the Divinely inspired prophet-revolutionaries, men of God, or righteous leaders of the poor, according to the Qur'an, had, in gerneral, three aims: first, to proclaim truth: secondly, to struggle against falsehood, *Batil,* and oppression, *Zulm*: and thirdly, to establish a community, or Brotherhood of social equality, goodness, justice and love.

Contrasting Moses and Pharaoh as two antithetical forces of goodness and evil, right and wrong, true and false, the Qur'an shows them to represent two antagonistic forces. The force of the rich and arrogant ruling classes and the force of the humble, poor and weak slaves, oppressed workers, widows, orphans and helpless human beings. In the end, the poor led by the prophets and their truth come out as victorious and the corrupt are vanquished. "We rehearse to thee (O Muhammad!) some of the story of Moses and Pharaoh in truth, for the people who believe (in truth). Truly Pharaoh elated himself in the land and broke up its people into groups and classes, making one class weak and oppressed among them: their sons he slew but he kept alive their females;

for he was indeed one of the corrupters (of the world). And We wished to be gracious to those who were being oppressed and were made weak and poor in the land, to make them leaders and make them heirs to establish a firm place for them in the land, and to show Pharaoh, Haman and their hosts, at their hands, the very things against which they were taking precautions." (28: 3–6).

The prophets' revolt was basically against the forces of iniquity, oppression and superstition. They rebelled against the powerful groups and classes which ruled over corrupt social orders. The prophet-revolutionaries were rebels and non-conformists who never compromised with evil and falsehood. They have many common traits, qualities, roles and characters.

They were all men of God, who led people to truth and social equality. They were courageous and righteous, noble and humble. They had bargained as revolutionaries their possessions, lives, material goods, wealth, comforts and privileges, talents and powers for a just social order of truth and equality. They sacrificed every thing for their cause. They were persecuted, humiliated and sometimes killed. They had to migrate to a new land from where they struggled to emancipate the oppressed and suffering human beings.

This is the Quranic concept of *Jihad*, the war for emancipating the poor and weak. In this war they remain steadfast, patient and constant and never swerve or compromise, deviate or waver:

"God hath purchased of the Believers," says the Qur'an," their persons and their goods; for theirs (in return) is the Garden: they fight in His cause and slay and are slain: a promise binding on Him in Truth, through the Torah, Evangel and the Qur'an. And who is more faithful to his Covenant than God? Then rejoice in the bargain which ye have concluded. That is the achievement supreme." (9: 111).

> "Those who believe (in truth and equality) and suffer exile and strive with might and main, in God's cause (of truth and equality) with their goods and their persons, have the highest rank in the sight of God: they are the people who will achieve (salvation). Their Lord doth give them glad tidings of a Mercy from Himself, of His good pleasure and of Gardens for them, wherein are delights that endure. They will dwell therein for ever. Verily, in God's presence is a reward, the greatest (of all) (9: 20–22).

2. The True Believers:

The Qur'an defines true believers (in truth and equality) in these words: "Those who believe and adopt exile, and fight for God's cause (of truth), as well as those who give (them) asylum and aid–these are (all) in very truth the Believers: for them is the forgiveness of sins and a provision most generous." (8: 74). And one who forsakes his hearth and home, his family and tribe, his wealth and possessions for the sake of his cause (of truth and equlity) "finds in the earth many a refuge, wide and spacious. Should he die as a refugee from home for God and His Apostle, his reward becomes due and sure with God. And God is Oft-forgiving, Most Merciful." (4: 100). "How many of the prophets fought (for the cause of truth), and with them (fought) many godly men? But they never lost heart. If they met with disaster in God's way, neither did they weaken (in will) nor give in. And God loves those who are firm and steadfast." (3: 146).

The prophets were mocked and rejected by those who denied truth and human equality and oppressed the poor and the weak with arrogance and brute force. "To them came apostles with clear signs," says the Qur'an about the ancient people of 'Ad, Thamud, and prophet Nuh's community, And they put their hands upto their mouths

> and said: we do deny (the mission) on which ye have been sent and we are really in suspicious (disquieting) doubt as to that to which ye invite us. Their apostles said: 'Is there a doubt about God, the Creator of the heavens and the earth? It is He who invites you, in order that He may forgive you your sins and give you respite for a term appointed! They said: 'Ah! ye are no more than human, like ourselves; ye wish to turn us away from (the institutions, gods, idols, and rituals), our fathers used to worship: then bring us some clear authority. Their apostles said to them: 'True we are human like yourselves but God doth grant His grace to such of His servants as He pleases. It is not for us to bring you an authority except as God permits. And on God let all men of faith put their trust. No reason have we why we should not put our trust on God. Indeed He has guided us to the ways we (follow). We shall certainly bear with patience all the hurt you may cause us. For those who put their trust should put their trust on God'. And those who rejected (truth) said to their apostles: 'Be sure we shall drive you out of our land, or ye shall return to our way of life, but their Lord inspired (this Message): verily We shall cause the oppressors to perish." (14: 9–13).

The highest value or principle for the prophets is to worship none but God, and trust none but Him. What does worship of God imply in moral and social terms?

Every prophet invited his contemporary people to worship God alone and join no partners with Him. (11: 25–49, 50–58, 61–68, 84–95, and 26: 70–104, 105–122, etc).

According to the Qur'an, the prophets worship God alone who is the source of all goodness, power, wisdom, knowledge and mercy. They fear Him and put all their trust on Him. And to seek help from men other than God or fear any one except God is *Shirk,* to join gods with God. *Shirk* is the most heinous sin and crime which makes human beings as worthless as a worm and as impotent and powerless as dust. The Qur'an compares the *Mushrik* (one who joins gods with God and fears them except Him) to a weightless thing fallen from the sky and devoured by the birds or thrown to a far off place. Such a person, all his life, runs after a mirage and dies of thirst. Associating gods with God is a great lie, a falsehood and a self–delusion which reduces man to the level of a worthless thing. A *Mushrik* has no centre or stability since he runs after gods of his own imagination and hankers after idols who cannot benefit or harm him. He lives in a vicious circle and revolves round material things and chattels of deception which, he wrongly thinks, will give him power and strength. *Shirk* is really falsehood and lie.

According to the Qur'an, God is the Creator and Nourisher of this universe. He plans and guides and governs the universe. He is full of power, mercy, goodness, knowledge and wisdom. The prophets submit their selves to the higher plan of God. This submission to the Divine will is literally called *Islam.* The prophets think, act and plan according to the Divine pleasure. They please none but God*; they seek help from Him and turn to Him in prosperity and adversity, in joy and sorrow, in pain and suffering. They have an intense awareness of God's presence. He protects them, sustains them and guides them.

The prophets do not follow their selfish desires, lusts and passions; they are selfless and are guided invisibly by the mighty hand of God. What the prophets follow is the truth. Those who seek help from mortal human beings, powerful kings, lords and priests and follow their lusts and selfish desires are those who join gods with God. Human lusts, passions, fancies, whims, superstitions, cults and rituals, idols of stone and wood, and idols of human flesh and blood are all gods whom ordinary and weak people worship. The *Mushriks* deny truth and "They only follow their own lusts; and who is more astray than one who follows his own lusts, devoid of guidance from God? For God guides not people who oppress (the weak)" (28: 50).

The theological conception of a Godhead is actually the conception of higher principles or values which sustain human life on this earth: truth, honesty, love, sincerity, goodness, justice, equality and brotherhood of human beings. The prophets fear only God and put trust on Him; that is, they dedicate their lives to proclaim truth and establish a social order based on these high principles, and values.

They struggle against those forces which divide mankind into warring factions, groups and classes, one class

---

* "And call not, besides God, on another god," says the Qu'ran to prophet Muhammad, "There is no god but He. Every thing (that exists) will perish except His own Face. To him belongs the Command, and to Him will ye (all) be brought back." (28: 88) "Behold", Luqman (the wiseman) said to his son by way of instruction: "O my son! Join not in worship (others) with God for *Shirk* or false worship is indeed the highest wrong-doing". (31: 13).

exploiting and oppressing the others. The prophets fight against iniquities, injustices, tyranny and oppression. They are fearless and selfless because they identify themselves with the high 'Divine' principles of truth, equality and brotherhood; their power is the natural, historical and 'Divine' power: They fight for the cause of the oppressed, the poor, weak and the downtrodden.

They struggle courageously and persevere and librerate suffering mankind from the slavery of oppressors, exploiters, lords, slave-owners and priests. They emancipate people from superstition, weaknesses, and imperfections produced by ***Shirk,*** fear, wild passions, selfishness, arrogance and lusts of material goods.

Shirk is the weakness and powerlessness which is the cause of all psychological, mental, social and moral diseases in individuals and societies. People start fearing and mistrusting each other. Those who do not trust God cease to trust themselves. They lose all faith in their own worth and abilities.

There is no good in their life but comes from God. To think otherwise and to attribute good to any human being, lord, king or chief is to set up false gods and idols. To think and act on such false notions is to become slave of men. It would then negate higher values of life. To submit to the higher will and plan of God and to the higher values and principles of truth, equality and justice which emanate from the higher Divine source, is the real freedom from lusts and temptations of evil, from slavery to material goods, false values and from slavery to powerful pharaohs, kings, lords and oppressors.

The hearts of the oppressors are always diseased. They judge the prophets with their own false standards. One who is not dishonest like them, and is on the contrary, a selfless, humble and honest man is insane bacause he does not run after material and worldly possessions: money, lands, houses, power and privileges and does not lie and exploit the poor. A man who deviates from their beaten path of dishonesty, iniquity, superstition and falsehood appears to them as a liar and a poet. "Their hearts play as with trifles. The oppressors conceal their private counsels (saying), 'Is this (one) more than a man like ourselves? Will ye go to witchcraft with your eyes open?' The prophet replied:' My Lord knoweth (every) word (spoken) in the heavens and on earth: He is the One that heareth and knoweth (all things). 'Nay' they said, (these are) medleys of dreams!– Nay, he forged it! Nay, he is (but) a poet: Let him then bring us a sign like the ones that were sent to (prophets) of old'! (As to those) before them, not one of the populations which We destroyed believed (in truth): Will these believe? (21: 3–6).

The oppressors reject the principles of truth, social equality, love and brotherhood for which the prophets stand and struggle all their lives. The oppressors, like the Egyptian Pharaoh, divide the iniquitous communities into classes of oppressors and oppressed. The powerful oppressors try to control all means of production and sources of sustenance in order to compel the masses to submit to their command. They tend to enslave and mislead the entire populations.

The prophet-revolutionaries seek to destroy such regimes of evil and oppression. All their energies, powers and talents are spent to abolish oppression (*Zulm*) in all its forms. The struggle between the forces of evil and goodness, iniquity and justice characterizes the antithesis between prophets and pharaohs, between the revolutionary leaders of the poor and the weak, and the chiefs of the oppressors and exploiters.

3. The Way of Truth:

In the end the higher values of truth and equality triumph over falsehood and iniquity, for the communities of oppressors are doomed to extinction. The prophet-revolutionaries follow the path of truth and righteousness. The way of life which they trod was that of Islam. But what is Islam? As we shall discuss this in another section of this book, we shall confine ourselves here to saying that, literally, Islam is surrender or submission of one's will to the Universal will and plan of God, of truth, goodness, power, justice and mercy. It is a complete dedication of oneself to these higher principles.

In this total submission the devotee, the man of God, the *Muslim,* surrenders him, and all his thoughts, motives, passions, emotions, desires, ideals, possessions to the will of God or the cause of truth for which he struggles all his life. The will of God or the natural and historical forces, govern phenomena of nature, society and history. All prophet-revolutionaries were *Muslims,* submitters to the will of God. "God opens the breast of a person for Islam, submission to God, whom, He wants to guide" (6: 125). "One who submits (*aslama*) his face to God and he is doer of good deeds, he is rewarded by God and such people have no fear, nor do they grieve." (2: 112; 31: 22).

When the prophets Ibrahim and Isma'il were rebuilding the fundations of Ka'ba in Mecca, they prayed to God in these words: "Our Lord make us submitters (*Muslimin*) i.e. a community which shall obey you (2: 128)". "Ibrahim was neither a Jew nor a Christian but a Hanif (follower of God's straight path of truth), submitting (to God) and was not one of those who obey beings other than God, i.e. associate others with God, *Mushriks*". (3: 67). Prophet Muhammad was a *Muslim*

(6: 163), among the Arabs. The latter had forgotten the original moral teachings of Ibrahim and had restricted their *din,* way of life, to mere superficial observance of rituals and cults (26: 70–104).

"Say, O prophet! shall I take for my protector any other than God, the Maker of the heavens and the earth? And He it is that feedeth but is not fed. Say: Nay! but I am commanded to be the first of those who surrender (to God) and be not thou of the company of those who join gods with God." (6: 14). "Is one whose heart God has opened to his submission (of His Will) so that he has received enlightenment from God, (no better than one hard-hearted)? Woe to those whose hearts are hardened against celebrating the praises of God. They are manifestly wandering (in error)" (39: 22).

Whenever the prophet-revolutionaries called upon the wrong-doers to give up their corrupt practices, ideas and institutions, they refused to do so. They could not part with their wealth and power and share them with the poor and the dispossessed: "Whenever We sent a warner before thee (O Muhammad!) to any people, the wealthy ones among them said: 'we found our fathers following a certain way of life and we will certainly follow in their footsteps'; he said: 'What even if I brought you better guidance than that which ye found your fathers following'? They said: 'for us, we deny that ye (prophets) are sent (on a mission at all)". (43: 23–24).

Right and wrong ways of life are clear to man, says the Qur'an. He may follow truth or falsehood. "Let there be no compulsion in the following (of right or wrong) way of life. Truth stands out clear from error. Whoever rejects evil and believes in God (i.e. Truth) has grasped the most trustworthy hand-hold that never breaks. And God heareth and knoweth all things. God is the protector of those who believe (in truth). From the depths of darkness He will lead them forth into light. Of those who reject truth their patrons are the Evil ones: From light they will lead them forth into the depths of darkness. They will be companions of the Fire, to dwell there in (for ever) (2: 256–257).

4. What is Zulm, Oppression?

The social end of prophets' struggle is elimination of oppression (*Zulm*) from the face of the earth. But what is oppression or *Zulm*? Literally, *Zulm* means to remove a thing from its rightful place, or to deprive a thing or person of its due share or right. *Zulm* is thus a disequilibrium, a disharmony, a deprivation, an imbalance or a disturbance in the natural order, harmony, or equilibrium of things.

A man who rejects truth, social equality or justice is a *Zalim,* an oppressor who denies higher values of harmonious and equal human life; he is a *Kafir,* who denies truth, equality (and God). A brute who uses naked force to kill the weak, is a *Zalim* or an oppressor who deprives another human being of his natural right to life and honour. A powerful class of oppressors who forcibly capture major means of production of society and reduce the broad masses to a life of bare subsistence, slavery and dependence are *Zalimun,* oppressors.

But let us see how the Qur'an defines *Zulm. Zalimun,* wrongdoers or oppressors are those who deny (God, truth, justice and equality) (2:254). They are "those who deny the Signs of God, and in defiance of right slay the prophets, and slay those who from among the people enjoin justice." (3:21). The Qur'an likens the state of oppressors to a harvest afflicted by biting frost. "Those who reject (truth and equality)—neither their possessions nor their (numerous) praying will avail them aught against God. They will be companions of the Fire dwelling therein for ever. What they spend in the life of this (material) world may be likened to a wind which brings a nipping frost, it strikes and destroys the harvest of men who have wronged their own souls. It is not God that hath wronged them, but they wrong themselves". (3: 116–117) "*Zalimun* are those who reject Our Signs and treat them with arrogance." (7: 40–41). These oppressors persecute the weak, *al-mustad'afun,* men, women and children in their oppressive social orders (4: 75). The oppressors hate truth and fight in the cause of evil (43: 78; 4: 74).

A derivative meaning of the word *Zulm* is to deprive a person of his due share or right, as in an exchange of goods between two persons one pays less to the other and thus gains an advantage over the other. Exchange is a broad term and may include various economic relationships and transactions between individuals, groups or classes. *Riba** is such a broad term used in the Qur'an.

In the pre-feudal society of the Hijaz, *riba* transactions involved loans of money, commodity, grains or cattle to the poor and needy people by the usurers and merchants who charged exorbitant rates of interest/usury, thus, devouring the entire properties of the poor people and tribes. In this transaction the wealthy merchants exploited the poor peasants, artisans and the needy. This exploitation of the poor is termed by the Qur'an as *Zulm*. "O ye who believe! fear God, and give up what remains of your demand for usury/interest, if ye are indeed believers (in truth and equality). If ye do it not,

---

* See for details, the present writer's work, *Islam and Feudalism: The Economics of Riba, Interest and Profit* (Lahore: Vanguard Books, 1985).

take notice of war from God and His Apostle: but if ye turn back ye shall have your capital sums. Deal not unjustly and ye shall not be dealt unjustly *(la tazlimun wa la tuzlamun*"). (2: 278–279).

Lease of land against money or in kind to a tenant-cultivator by an absentee landlord was also termed an unjust exchange transaction in early Islam. The prophet-revolutionary of Islam had declared such leasing of land (*muzara'a*) unlawful.[1]

This means that all transactions in which an individual, group or class is defrauded, or exploited is *Zulm*. The forms, contents, methods and frameworks of perpetuating tyranny and oppression over a weak person or class have changed from pre-feudal times of seventh century Mecca to the modern economic system of capitalism.

The cruelty and exploitation of slaves by a slave-owner and systematic and organized exploitation of today's industrial and agricultural labourers by powerful capitalists and landlords are different forms of *Zulm*. Now, under capitalism, the ruling capitalists combine to take over means of production, state structures and apparatuses to suppress and exploit the working classes.

According to the Qur'an, God is the source of all goodness, power, wisdom and knowledge. All that is good emanates from Him. If a person does not believe this he 'worships' a false God which may be a powerful rich person, king, a feudal lord, or rite, custom, institution, idol, fancy, caprice or any imaginary thing or a superstition. If any person starts adoring his own self, and attributing all earned wealth, knowledge, wisdom, power, honour and prestige due to his own abilities and talents, knowledge and wisdom, he sets up himself as a god. He be-

1. *Landlord and Peasant in Early Islam* (Islamabad: Islamic Research Institute, 1977: reprint 1984).

comes arrogant, proud, insolent and hard-hearted. Such a person is a *Zalim* or oppressor of his own self.

Therefore those who reject (God and) higher values of truth, social equality, brotherhood, love, humility, justice and goodness are oppressors, because, they divide their societies into powerful and weak, rich and poor and set up social order of iniquity, injustice and oppression.

The prophet-revolutionaries stand for truth, equality and justice and they declare war against all sorts of oppressors, exploiters, tyrants, falsifiers and liars. And God never guides those who oppress, and exploit the poor and weak:

> "It was not We that wronged them (the oppressors). They wronged their own souls. The gods other than God whom they invoked,profited them no whit when there issued the decree of thy Lord. Nor did they add aught (to their lot) but perdition. Such is the chastisement of thy Lord when He chastises communities which oppress (the weak). Grievous, indeed, and severe is His chastisement." (11: 101–102).
>
> "Do they not travel through the earth, and see what was the end of those before them? They were superior to them in strength: they tilled the soil and populated it in great numbers than these have done. There came to them their apostles with clear (Signs), (which they rejected to their own destruction): it was not God who wronged them, but they wronged their own selves" (30: 9).

The Qur'an compares the communities of oppressors to spider's web. Like the flimsy web of the spider, the social orders based on evil, oppression and exploitation of the large masses are weak and unstable. (29: 41).

4

THE PROPHET–REVOLUTIONARIES AND THE PROLETARIAT.

The prophet-revolutionaries lead the proletariat, the weak, the dispossessed, the poor (*aradhil, mustad-'afun*) against the powerful rich (*mutrafun, mustakbarun, mala'a*). Because of this struggle the old social order splits up into these two broad polarized classes of the rich and the poor. The prophets and their proletariat believe in truth and social equality. The rich reject truth and social equality because their old social order is based on oppression of the poor proletariat whom they mercilessly exploit and persecute.

The prophets and their followers love truth and equality more than any thing else, more than their families and possessions: "O ye who believe! Take not for protectors your fathers and your brothers if they love rejection (of truth) above faith (in truth): if any of you do so, they do wrong. Say (O prophet!): If it be that your fathers, your sons, your brothers, your mates, or your kindred; the wealth that ye have gained; the commerce in which ye fear a decline; or the dwellings in which ye delight–are dearer to you than God (i.e. truth), or His Apostle, or the striving in His cause;– then wait until God brings about His Decision: and God guideth not the wicked people". (9: 23–24).

1. Proletariat and their Persecution:

The proletariat is persecuted by the powerful rich because of the former's cause of truth and equality, whereas the latter perpetuate falsehood and inequality. They oppress and hate the poor slaves, workers, women and orphans, who find no place in the social order of iniquity. The prophets lead them and protect them from oppression and brutality. "The chiefs of those who rejected (truth and equality) among his (Nuh's) people said: 'We see in thee nothing but a man like ourselves; nor do we see, that any follow thee but the meanest among us, *aradhiluna,* in judgement immature, nor do we see in you (all) any merit above us; infact we think ye are liars". (11: 27; see also, 26: 111).

The proletariat, in due course of time, becomes a brotherehood of truth, and a community of believers who sever their relations with the old iniquitous social order in which they are looked down upon as outcastes, as abominable creatures since they develop a new moral criterion of judging things according to the guidance provided by their divinely inspired prophet-revolutionary. Their struggle against the forces of evil shakes them up in wars against the oppressors.

When the proletariat, the slaves and workers are oppressed, persecuted and humiliated, they face all odds courageously and break all relations with the old corrupt order, give up their hearths and homes, families and tribes for the sake of truth for which they fight. They move away from the citadel of evil and oppression:

> "When angels take the souls of those who die in persecution and oppression, they say: In what (plight) were ye? They reply: 'weak and oppressed were we in the earth.' They say, 'was not the earth

of God spacious enough for you to move yourselves away (from evil)? Such men will find their abode in Hell,– what an evil refuge!– except those who are (really) weak and oppressed–men, women, and children–who have no means in their power, nor (a guide-post) to direct their way. For these there is hope that God will forgive; for God doth blot (sins) and forgive again and again. He who forsakes his home in the cause of God, finds in the earth many a refuge wide and spacious; should he die as a refugee from home for God and His Apostle his reward becomes due and sure, with God. And God is Oft-forgiving, Most Merciful". (4: 97–100)

The Qur'an divides the contemporary Arab people, in general, in two broad groups: those who are rich, powerful and arrogant (*mustakbarun)*, and those who are weak, poor and oppressed, *mustad'afun*. (4: 75–76; 7: 75–76). The former reject truth and social equality and the latter tend to believe in truth and social equality. The rich rulers covet material power, they pile up wealth and accumulate material goods and aspire to command armies of people. They follow vanities and false standards to judge things and matters. They value pride, greed, naked force, selfishness, fraud and deception because their entire social order is based on oppression and deception of the poor working classes of slaves and artisans. The poor are persecuted and maltreated as animals.

The poor, the proletariat, are those who do not possess anything but their physical power and brains. They find refuge with the prophet-revolutionary who treats them as equal human beings, honourable and worthy of all respect. With him they find true humanity, real equality, justice and brotherhood, love and mercy. They leave their masters, abandon their fields of work, throw away their burdens and refuse to be the beasts of burden. They revolt against the old social order This revolt of the poor poses a danger to the decadent social order and a threat to the status-quo. The rich slave-owners and lords ask the prophet-revolutionary to disown his proletariat, disband them and surrender them to their owners and lords. But he refuses to do so:

> "Send not away," says the Qur'an to Muhammad, "those who call on their Lord morning and evening seeking His face (or pleasure). You are not responsible for what they do, nor are they accountable to what you do, that thou shouldst turn them away and thus be (one) of the oppressors. Thus did We try some of them by comparison with others that they (the rich) should say: is it these (proletariat) then that God hath favoured from among us?' Doth not God know best those who are grateful (for His bounties)". (6: 52–53).

2. Prophets and proletariat:

The prophet-revolutionaries were of low social origins; most of them belonged to the poor working classes and earned their living from honest means, with thier own labour. Nuh was probably a teacher and a carpenter. Musa was a shephered. Shu'ayb and Hud were poor teachers. Ibrahim was a mason; 'Isa was a carpenter. Muhammad was a shepherd and a labourer. Actually, the prophets worked with their own hands, believed in the dignity of labour and honest living. They knew many crafts and most of them were workers and artisans. They rose from humble and ordinary positions as sincere leaders and teachers of the humble, poor and downtrodden slaves and workers, and suffered and lived like them. They depended on their own productive labour and legitimate means of sustenance.

They were themselves the members of the poor proletariat. As honest and sincere men, they were truthful in their beliefs, deeds, words and actions. Whatever they thought, did or acted was truth. Truth is not double-faced. They believed in social equality. Therefore they considered themselves humble members of the proletariat. They respected other people as equals, because in the Brotherhood of Equality are all equal and honourable, no one is low or high, lord or slave.

In the 'Brotherhood of Equality' only those mattered who were truthful, sincere, honest, bold and courageous. There was no difference between the leader and the follower revolutionaries. Pride, arrogance, falsehood, greed and lust have no place in their Brotherhood.

> "O ye apostles; enjoy (all) things good and pure, and do good deeds, for I am wel acquainted with (all) that ye do, and verily, this Brotherhood of yours is a single Brotherhood, and I am your Lord and Cherisher: Therefore fear Me (and no other). But people have cut off their affair (of unity) between them, into sects; each party rejoices in that which is with itself . . ." (23: 51–54).

The Qur'an reminds the early Muslim revolutionaries of the times when they were a weak and small group of rebels, an insignificant band of poor slaves and workers, a proletariat, humiliated and persecuted in Mecca when their very lives, their families, their wealth and honour were all in danger. Many were killed and many were exiled.

And ultimately they escaped to Medina where they

organized themselves into an armed force of truth and equality, and at last succeeded in liberating Mecca and the rest of Arabia from oppression, injustice and superstitious religion:

> "And remember when ye were a small (band), despised through the land, and afraid that men might despoil and kidnap you; but He provided a safe asylum for you, strengthened you with His aid, and gave you good things for sustenance, that ye might be grateful.
> O ye that believe ! Betray not the trust of God and the Apostle, nor misappropriate knowingly things entrusted to you. And know ye that your possessions and your children are but a trial; and that it is God with whom lies your highest reward." (8: 26–28).

The prophet-revolutionary identifies himself with his followers who give up everything for the sake of truth, equality and justice and strive hard to found a community of equality and brotherhood. He is one of the revolutionaries, he is a leader, but he is not above them; he is equal to them. Like everyone else he is responsible for his acts. Like them, he does not amass wealth, nor does he enjoy exclusive privileges. He is just like them: humble, ordinary, selfless and sincere.

Nuh was a great prophet-revolutionary, and a man of truth who rejected the evil order of his contemporary community. He refused to disband and handover the poor slaves and workers who gathered around him. His address to his corrupt community excellently illustrates and underlines the point of view of the prophet–revolutionaries and their devotion to the proletariat:

> "And O my people," said Nuh to the rich leaders and chiefs of his community, "I ask you for no

wealth in return; my reward is from none but God. But I will not drive away (in contempt) those who believe. For verily they are to meet their Lord and ye I see are the ignorant ones! And O my people! who would help me against God if I drove them away? Will ye not then take heed?"

"I tell you not that with me are treasures of God nor do I know what is hidden, nor claim I to be an angel. Nor yet do I say, of those whom your eyes do despise that God will not give them wealth. God knowest best what is (hidden) in their souls. I should if I did, indeed be a wrong-doer." (11: 29–31).

Before the revelation of truth, inspiration and enlightenment come to the prophet, evil, sin and corruption sap the vigour and vitality of the people and weaken their moral, spiritual and intellectual faculties. Most men and women almost die in the moral sense as they lose deirection and purpose of their life and existence. They drift aimlessly. And because of general depravity and degeneration they fall victims to temptations, greed, lust, arrogance, selfishness, pride, falsehood, and corrupt ways of life. This is death. This is end of fellowfeeling, love and compassion for others. People become self-centred, selfish and mean. They become hard-hearted like stones, and callous like animals, nay, worse than animals. (25: 44).

With the revelation, truth and guidance the prophets instill a new spirit and a new life in the 'dead' people and revive them. The Qur'an uses the simile of rain for revelation. As rain brings life to a dead and barren land, similarly revelation brings life to a 'dead' people:

"It is God who sends the winds and they raise the clouds: then does He spread them in the sky as He wills, and break them into fragments, until thou seest rain-drops issue from the midst thereof: then when He has made them reach such of His servants as He wills, behold, they do rejoice. Even though before they received (the rain) just before this – they were dumb with despair!– Then contemplate (O man!) the memorials of God's Mercy: How He gives life to the earth after its death: verily, the same will give life to the men who are dead; for He has power over all things". (30: 48–50).

"And among His signs is this: thou seest the earth barren and desolate; but when We send down rain to it, it is stirred to life and yields increase. Truly, He who gives life to the (dead) earth can surely give life to (people) who are dead, for He has power over all things. (41: 39).

After regaining their lost vigours, powers, talents and abilites the proletariat becomes an invincible force of truth. They imbibe in them, like their leader, the higher principles and values of truth, equality, honesty, brotherhood, love and sincerity. They become the 'Brotherhood of truth', and stand courageously against evil, oppression and falsehood. They struggle with their might and main against the forces of evil.

In this struggle against oppression they are cleansed of imperfections and are purified of weaknesses:

"And if any strive (with might and main) they do so for their own selves: for God is free of all needs from all creation. Those who believe and work righteous deeds–from them shall We blot out all evil (that may be) in them, and We shall reward them according to the best of their deeds" (29: 6–7).

Moreover, in the proletariat which is led by the prophet-revolutionary, there may be some hypocrites, or weak spirits. Without testing their faith and convictions in a war or struggle the sincere and true ones cannot be distinguished from the insincere and hyporcrites:

> "Do men think that they will be left alone on saying 'We believe and that they will not be tested? We did test those before them, and God will certainly know those who are true from those who are false. "(29: 2–3).
>
> "And God most certainly knows those who believe, and as certainly those who are hypocrites."
>
> "And the unbelievers say to those who believe 'Follow our path, and we will bear (the consequences) of your faults (and weaknesses)'. Never in the least will they bear their faults: in fact they are liars". (29: 11–12).

5

THE CONCEPTS OF JIHAD, HIJRA AND SOCIAL EQUALITY.

The main task of the prophet-revolutionaries was to establish truth, justice and an equalitarian social order in place of oppression and iniquity to distinguish right from wrong, just from unjust, good from evil, and true from false:

> "We sent Our prophets with clear Signs and sent down with them the Book and the Balance (of Right and Wrong), that men may stand forth in justice; and We sent down iron in which is (material for) mighty war, as well as many benefits for mankind, that God may test who it is that will help, unseen, Him and His apostles: for God is full of strength, Exalted in Might (and able to enforce His will) (57: 25).

1. Revelation, Justice and War:

Three things, revelations, justice and war for the supremacy of truth are the three important elements of the career and mission of a prophet-revolutionary. He discovers truth when revelation dawns on his mind and heart. In the light of this revelation and guidance he wages war against oppression and evil and struggles to establish a just social order of truth and social equality.

Jihad, war, and *Hijra* (migration), are the tactics and strategy of struggle and war for the cause of a just and equalitarian social order.

When the prophet-revolutionaries revolted against those corrupt orders they were persecuted, humiliated, exiled and even killed. They had to leave their homes, families and tribes. Under these circumstances their foremost task and strategy was to organize, strengthen and defend the helpless, weak and poor proletariat.

According to the Qur'an, the prophets' social mission was Islam, which is submission of human will to the will of God and direction of human conduct in accordance wth divine pleasure and plan. This is the religious-theological conception. In the social terms, Islam implies striving for this cause in this world in order to establish a just and equalitarian society. Islam is the Brotherhood of truth and equality. This is the end. *Jihad* is the means, method, plan and strategy to endeavour for such an order of equality, justice and goodness. This was the aim of prophets' missions in the pre-industrial society. And this was the purpose of the peophet-revolutionary, Muhammad.

The original concept of *Jihad* has been grossly misinterpreted by vested interests to advance their selfish and erroneous motives. The original meaning of *Jihad* was to struggle and strive for the cause of truth.

There were actually three phases of the Qur'anic concept and idea. First, it originated during a prolonged fight against the forces of evil, as struggle for truth, justice and equality for the downtrodden, poor, and weak individualş, groups, classes and tribes of the Hijaz, in the early decades of the seventh century A.D. Secondly, *Jihad* constituted a method for emancipating the oppressed artisans, slaves, women, and orphans from the tyranny of slave-owners, usurer-merchants, priests and chiefs. Thridly, the objective of the struggle for emancipating the weak was to establish a social order of equality. *Jihad* was thus a continuous, neverceasing struggle against the forces of oppression, injustice and inequality:

> "And why should ye not fight in the cause of God," says the Qur'an to the early Muslim revolutionaries, "and of those, who being weak, are oppressed–men, women and children, whose cry is: 'Our Lord: rescue us from this town, whose people are oppressors; and raise for us from Thee one who will protect; and raise for us from Thee who will help: Those who believe (in truth) fight in the cause of God, and those who reject (truth) fight in the cause of evil: so fight ye against the friends of Satan: feeble indeed is the cunning of Satan".(4: 75–76).

Literally, *jahada* means to struggle, strive and fight. *Jihad* is the striving and fight for some cause." And strive, *Jahidu,* in God's cause as ye ought to strive (with sincerity and under discipline)." (22: 78). "Do not listen to those who reject (God, truth) but strive against them with the utmost strenuousness with the (Qur'an)" (25: 52). "And those who strive in Our (cause), We will certainly guide them to Our paths, for verily God is with those who do right". (29: 69).

Those who fight for truth and social equality with dedication and sincerity are superior to those who perpetuate an unjust social order and pay only lip service to the higher values of truth and morality. The Qur'an reprimands and questions the hypocrisy of the arrogant Qureshite merchants and priests who considered external hypocritical rites equal to higher values of truth, sincerity and justice:

"Do ye make the giving of drink to pilgrims and the

maintenance of the sacred Mosque, equal to (the pious service) of those who believe in God (i.e. values of truth, justice and goodness), and the Last Day, and strive, (*jahada*), with might and main in the cause of God? They are not comparable in the sight of God: and God guides not those who oppress (the poor). Those who believe and suffer exile and strive with might and main in God's cause with their wealth and their persons have the higher ranks in the sight of God: They are the people who will achieve (salvation)". (9: 19–20).

The slaves, women, orphans, workers and young people who accepted and believed in the mission of justice and equality were persecuted, exiled or killed. A time comes when this proletariat takes up arms to defend themselves, the new ideas and the new community, and its new way of life:

> "Will ye not fight people who violated their oaths, plotted to expel the Apostle and took the aggressive by being the first (to assault) you. Do you fear them? Nay, it is God whom you should more justly fear, if ye believe (in truth)". (9: 13).

The Muslim revolutionaries are exhorted to wage a relentless war against those who reject truth and equality, but they should restrain them and must not commit excesses. Their objective is to destroy the forces of oppression, injustice and cruelty to pave the way for a just society:

> "Fight in the cause of God, those who fight you, but not transgress limits, for God loveth not transgressors. And slay them wherever ye catch them, and turn them out from where they have turned you out; for persecution and oppression (*Fitna*) are worse than slaughter; but fight them not at the sacred Mosque, unless they (first) fight you there.

> But if they fight you, slay them. Such is the reward of those who reject (truth). But if they cease, God is Oftforgiving, Most Merciful. And fight them on until there is no more oppression and there prevail (justice and truth) God's way of life. But if they cease, let there be no hostility except to those who practise oppression. "(2: 190–193).

Jihad, or the war against oppression and inequality is necessary to protect the 'Brotherhood of Truth and Equality' which the revolutionaries establish when they revolt against the combined forces of slave-owners, usurers-merchants, usurpers, priests, lords and chiefs. They have to continue their struggle and fight until the social order of truth and equality prevails over the oppressors' corrupt ways of life, institutions, and practices.

There cannot be any compromise with oppression because whenever the corrupt rulers find any opportunity or slackness on the part of the revolutionaries they will try to annihilate them, for revolutionaries' death is oppressors' life. As both oppression and revolution (for truth, justice and equality) are contradictions, persecution and oppression (*Fitna*) of the revolutionaries is worse than death: it is slavery, and slavery is neither life nor death. Therefore, without waging war (*Jihad*) for the sake of truth and justice, no revolution can be defended, saved and protected. *Jihad* or continuous war against evil is necessary.

In the early and late medieval times, and very often in the modern age, this Quranic idea of *Jihad* (of the oppressed proletariat) has been misinterpreted and even distorted by autocrats and usurpers who misused it for their own political and economic ends. It is wrongly taken as a 'holy war' against their political adversaries. Not only the idea of *Jihad* but also the concepts of *salat* and *Zakat* have been misinterpreted by the rulers, lords, chiefs and priests for political purposes, for conserving the feudal social relations and institutions of slavery, serfdom, monarchy and systematic exploitation of the working classes.

The pristine idea, the original concept of *Jihad* was the life-and-death struggle of the oppressed and exploited slaves and the poor—the wretched of the earth—to save their social revolution from the onslaught of the oppressors and exploiters of all sorts. Their persecution and oppression at the hands of the hard-hearted slave-owners, lords, priests and chiefs of the *Hijaz* was so severe and brutal that it was considered worse than slaughter.

So the Qur'an enjoins upon the persecuted proletariat to fight against their oppressors (*Zalimun*) who are bent upon destroying the just and equalitarian society of the revolutionaries.

> "To those against whom war is made (by the oppressors) permission is given (to fight) because they are oppressed;– and verily, God is more Powerful for their aid;– (they are) those who have been expelled from their homes in defiance of right (for no cause) except that they say, 'Our Lord is God'; Did not God check one set of people by means of another, there would surely have been pulled down monasteries, churches, synagogues and mosques, in which the name of God is commemorated in abundant measure. God will certainly aid those who aid His (cause);– for verily God is full of strength, Exalted in Might, (able to enfore His Will). (They are) those who if We establish them in the land, establish *salat* and give *Zakat*, enjoin the right and forbid wrong; with God rests the end (and decision) of (all) affairs." (22: 39–41).

And God helps the cause of truth, justice and equality and destroys the forces of oppression and evil. "Nay We hurl the truth against falsehood, and it knocks out its brain, and behold, falsehood doth perish; Ah! woe be to you for the (false) things ye ascribe (to us)." (21: 18).

2. Prophets and Jihad:

According to the genuine traditions of the prophet-revolutionary Muhammad, therefore, *Jihad* was accorded high priority in the Muslim Community. He is reported to have said: "I love to wage war in the cause of God and be killed, then to be brought to life and again be killed, again to be brought to life and again to be killed. He repeated it three times."[1]

In another tradition 'Ata' Ibn Yasar reports that the Prophet told them: "Should not I tell you about the best of men in reward and status: he is that who takes up the rein of his horse and fights in the cause of God? Should not I tell you the best of men in reward and status after him; he is that who grazes his small flock of sheep in a remote place and establishes *salat* and gives *Zakat* and worships God and does not join gods with Him?"[2]

In these reports *Jihad, salat and Zakat* are *emphasized* as three principles of the early Islam, and *Jihad* is considered superior to both formal *salat* and *Zakat* because without *Jihad* or constant struggle to defend the community no social and economic system can be established.

Under feudalism and monarchy when truth, justice and equality were sacrificed and iniquity and slavery were restored, *Jihad* as a defense strategy was neglected and a new political formula was invented which propagated to

1. Malik ibn Anas, *Muwatta'*, I, Kitab al-jihad.
2. Ibid.

the common people that Islam was built on five pillars: verbal affirmation of God and His apostle, establishment of formal *salat*, payment of legal *Zakat*, regular fasting for one month and annual pilgrimage to Mecca. There was no mention of *jihad* any more. No scientific investigation has been made as to ascertain the reasons for discarding *jihad* as the first and foremost principle of the Muslim Community, and for rigidifying *salat* and *Zakat* as formal and legalistic rituals devoid of high values of equality, truth and justice.

3. The Concept of Hijra in the Qur'an:

Literally *hijra* means migration from one place to another; it implies giving up or renunciation of one's hearth and home, family, land and nation, and all material goods and chattels which man covets, for some cause. It is a movement for a higher aim, the culminating point or the peak of struggle (*Jihad*) when those fighting for a new order of truth and human equality reject the old order of iniquity and corruption in order to accelerate their struggle against the evil forces of the old order.

The point of Hijra lies between the borders and lines of the old order and the new order not only on the physical-geographical plane but also on the social, economic, psychological, cultural, intellectual and civilizational planes because this point heralds the death of the old, decrepit, corrupt, divided and unequal world, and the birth of a vigorous, just and equalitarian new world.

It is a movement from immorality to morality, from falsehood to truth and from darkness to light. And a *Muhajir* is thus a person who is devoted to truth. He is a a man of principles and a revolutionary. He is resolute and courageous and does not compromise with evil and does not slacken his endeavours. Revolution is dear to his heart and for this reason alone he revolts against the corruption and oppression of the old social order.

He is dedicated exclusively to the cause of truth, justice, equality, liberty, love and brotherhood. Hijra is the dividing line between these contrasts and contradictions, between death and life, between slavery and freedom, between inequality and equality. The Qur'an says to the early Muslim revolutionaries:

> "O ye who believe! take not for protectors your fathers and your brothers if they prefer rejection (of truth) to belief (in truth): if any of you do so, they do wrong. Say: if it be that your fathers, your sons, your brothers, your mates, or your kindred, the wealth that ye have gained; the commerce in which ye fear a decline; or the dwellings in which ye delight—are dearer to you than God or His Apostle, or the striving in His cause:– then wait until God brings about His Decision: and God guideth not the corrupt people." (9: 23–24).

One who believes in higher values to which the whole struggle is dedicated must be ready for sacrifices of home, wealth, family and even life:

"Those who believe, and suffer exile and strive with might and main, in God's cause with their goods and their persons have the highest rank in the sight of God: they are the people who will achieve (salvation). Their Lord doth give them glad tidings of a Mercy from Himself, of His good pleasure, and of Gardens for them, wherein are delights that endure. They will dwell therein for ever. Verily in God's presence is a reward, th greatest (of all)". (9: 20–22).

According to the Qur'an, the prophets and their revolutionary followers love their cause more than anything else: they struggle for truth and justice. But the wrong-doers (*Zalimun*), the hard-hearted and corrupt rejected their message of love and equality. And the unbelievers said to their apostles: "Be sure we shall drive you out of our land, or ye shall return to our (old), way of life (*Milla*), but their Lord inspired to them: Verily We shall cause the wrong-doers to perish. And verily We shall cause you to abide in the land and succeed them. This for such as fear the Time when they stand before My Tribunal,–such as fear the punishment denounced." (14: 13–14).

Whenever the oppressors threatened or conspired to destroy the righteous who fought for truth and equality, they had compulsorily to migrate and leave their homes, tribes and communities behind. The Qur'an illustrates this point in a beautiful style, in its contemporary religious-theological mode:

> "When angels take the souls of those who die in oppression (without resisting it), they say: 'in what (plight) were ye'? They reply: 'weak and oppressed were we in the earth. They say: was not the earth of God spacious enough for you to move yourselves away (from evil)?' Such men will find their abode in Hell,–what an evil refuge! except those who are (really) weak and oppressed–men, women and children who have no means in their power, nor (a guide-post)to direct their way, for these, there is hope that God will forgive: for God doth blot (sins) and forgive again and again" (4: 97–98).

It means that if the rebels do not migrate and renounce their homes, wealth, and privileges, families and relations, old customs and depraved values and institutions, they will either be killed, destroyed or sucked into the pestering pores and sores of the corrupt and false society. If they migrate, organize and intensify their noble struggle against the forces of evil, they will be rewarded with victories beyond their expectations because God, natural, historical and moral forces will be on their side:

> "He who forsakes his home in the cause of God (i.e. truth and human equality) finds in the earth many a refuge wide and spacious. Should he die as a refugee from home for God and His Apostle, his reward becomes due and sure with God: and God is oft-forgiving, Most Merciful. "(4: 100).

The Qur'an says that almost all prophets had to leave their old homes, families and communities and migrate to other places for the sake of their cause of truth. This is the way of God *(Sunnat Allah)* which cannot be changed. Prophet Ibrahim had to leave his country Chaldea in Mesopotamia and migrate to Syria and Palestine. Prophet Musa left Egypt for Sinai Peninsula, and prophet Muhammad left Mecca and migrated to Yathrib with his followers in A.D. 622 when the powerful Meccan oligarchy of merchants, usurers, tribal chiefs, lords, slave-owners and priests conspired to destroy him.

This migration was for the cause of truth, human equality and justice and this was obviously against the corrupt social classes and groups of the old order: "But (prophet) Lot believed in Him. He said: I will leave home for the sake of my Lord: for He is Exalted in might, and Wise. . . He said to his people: ye do commit lewdness such as no people in creation (even) committed before you. Do ye indeed approach men, and cut off the highway? and practise wickedness (even) in your councils? But his people gave no answer but this: they said: 'Bring us the wrath of God if thou tellest the truth (29: 26–29).

"And his people gave no answer but this: they said; 'Drive them out of your community. These are indeed men who want to be clean and pure" (7: 80–82).

The prophet-revolutionaries faced similar situations when the arrogant and rich rulers of the oppressors' communities warned them: either they have to compromise with their evil ways or they must leave their communities:

> "The arrogant leaders of his community said: O Shuayb; we shall certainly drive thee out of our community (thee) and those who believe with thee; or else ye (thou and they) shall have to return to our way of life (*millat*). He said: 'What! even though we do detest (them)? (7: 88).

This shows that Hijra is not only giving up of home, family and old society, it is actually renunciation of all relations of blood, family, tribe, cultic religion, superstition, wealth, origin, status, power, pride and privilege (which are based on the system of oppression and exploitation) for the sake of one's cause of truth. Hijra is therefore the beginning of the brotherhood of truth, a fraternity of equality, justice and love–a paradise on earth.

The old ties, the conventional family, tribal, social and property relations which are not based on truth and equality, on common joys and sufferings are sundered and severed. This is the reason that this Brotherhood of truth cuts brother from brother, father from son and husband from wife because the new order, the new community is founded on the principles of truth, social equality, brotherhood and justice.

The members of this Brotherhood are those who speak the truth, are humble, courageous, and consider others as their equal, and are united in their fight against oppression and evil. They do not exploit and oppress each other.

Any liberated community of truth and equality cannot survive amidst formidable and evil forces of oppression if it does not defend and protect it from the aggressive attacks and sinister conspiracies of the exploiting classes whom the revolutionaries overthrow. Hijra and Jihad constitute the necessary tactics and strategy to safeguard the new community and its institutions. The Qur'an says:

> "O Ye who believe (in truth and equality)! what is the matter with you, then when ye are asked to go forth in the cause of God, ye cling heavily to the earth? Do you prefer the life of this world (the old evil order) to the Hereafter (the new order coming later)? But small are material goods of this life, as compared with the Hereafter. Unless ye go forth, He will punish you with a grievous penalty, and put others in your place; but Him ye would not harm in the least. For God hath power over all things" (9: 38–39).

This Quranic verse refers to the battle of Tabuk (9/631) in which the Muslims were led by the prophet Muhammad himself. But the significance of this verse is general. The revolutionaries who fight for the cause of truth, equality and justice must respond to the call of duty. If they lag behind, the enemy will take opportunity and will try to destroy the revolution and its cause.

This means that making of revolution is not enough: it must be protected and defended ceaselessly. When the call for the battle of Tabuk was made some Muslims hesitated. Their hearts were in the material goods. They wanted to harvest the fruit crop which was ripe. Some were afraid of the intense heat and long distance of the battle field. And the stern warning came:

> "Go ye forth, (whether equipped) lightly or heavily, and strive and struggle with your goods and your persons, in the cause of God. That is best for you, if ye (but) knew." (9: 41).

4. The Brotherhood of Equality:

The community which the revolutionaries establish after defeating the forces of oppression is the community of truth, equality and justice. It is the opposite of the community of the oppressors. It is a just and equalitarian social order which is built up in place of the old order of iniquity and injustice, slavery and bondage:

> O Ye who believe; stand out firmly for justice, as witnesses to God, even as against yourselves, or your parents, or your kin, and whether it be (against) rich or poor; for God can best protect both. Follow not the lusts (of your hearts), lest ye swerve, and if ye distort (justice) or decline to do justice, verily God is well-acquainted with all that ye do." (4: 135).

The Quranic words for justice (*'adl, qist,*) and goodness (*ihsan, birr, ma'ruf* etc) are broad and comprehensive in meaning. In the social sense they signify social equality as well as social justice. Social justice and social equality negate the existence of social classes based on economic and social differences and disparities. It further implies the social ownership of the major means of production and thus equal development of all.

As a social revolution levels down all economic and social differences and contrasts, the new social order fundamentally aims at an equal society in the sense that the groups and classes which oppress and exploit the weak sections of the community are suppressed or eliminated. In all its forms, *Zulm* (oppression, wrong-doing) is abolished. The revolutionaries encourage the moral qualities of truth, courage, brotherhood, equality, humility and struggle against the forces of evil. They discourage falsehood, injustice, selfishness, greed and exploitation:

> "God commands justice, the doing of good and generosity to kith and kin, and He forbids all shameful deeds, and injustice and corruption. He instructs you that ye may receive admonition. Fulfil the Covenant of God when ye have entered into it, and break not your oaths after ye have confirmed them: indeed ye have made God your surety: for God knoweth all that ye do. And be not like a woman who breaks into untwisted strands the yarn which she has spun after it has become strong. Nor take your oaths to practise deception between yourselves, lest one party should be more numerous than another; for God will test you by this; and on the Day of Judgement He will certainly make clear to you (the truth of) that wherein ye disagree." (16: 91–92).

> "We sent aforetime Our apostles with Clear Signs and sent down with them the Book and the Balance (*al-Mizan*) (of Right and Wrong), that men may stand forth in justice (*Qist*)". . . . (57: 25).

Justice means giving to each person, group, or class its due in order to maintan a balance or harmony in society. In the Just social order of the revolutionaries all are equal and they share all natural resources, and means of production in common. Nobody has the power and means to enslave others and exploit their labour power.

Justice is one of the higher values or principles which

govern the social order of equality. The other higher values are truth, honety; sincerity, selflessness, brotherhood and love. Justice is a principle derived from the higher Divine source. According to the Qur'an, the source of Justice, goodness, mercy, power, wisdom and knowledge is God. This means that everyone is subject to these principles. None is above them. Justice ought to be done irrespective of the status, position or power of a person. All are equal and all are free. Every one is responsible for his acts. None will bear the burden of others. Offices and rewards will go to those who deserve and are qualified. Everything is decided on merit.

In the Brotherhood of Truth or the community of equality all are equal: "Verily this Brotherhood of yours is a single Brotherhood, and I am your Lord and Cherisher. Therefore serve Me (and no other)." (21: 92 and 23: 52). "But people have cut off their affair of (unity), between them, into sects, and classes: each group rejoices in that which is with itself. But leave them in their confused ignorance for a time. Do they think that because We have granted them abundance of wealth and sons, We would hasten then on in every good? Nay, they (unbelievers) do not understand". (23: 53–56).

Those who reject truth and social equality and run after worldly wealth, power and material possessions to oppress the weak and poor and thus divide a community into antagonistic classes and groups, fall into self-deception and weakness.

On the other hand those who believe in truth and equality

> "are verily those who live in awe for fear of their Lord (abiding in the high principles of goodness, justice and equality); those who believe in the Signs of their Lord: those who join not (in worship)

partners with their Lord: and those who give away (to the needy) what they are given, with their hearts full of fear because they will return to their Lord;– it is these who hasten in every good work, and these who are foremost in them" (23: 57–61).

In the Brotherhood of Equality, therefore, all are equal and free. The well-being of an individual is dependent on the well-being of all. All are one and one is all. They have common hopes, aspirations, ideals, weals, and woes. They all adhere to the higher values, believe in them and act upon them. This transcendental reference to the higher values and principles is a binding force which gives stability, strength, purpose and direction to life and society. The believers live under the banner of truth and equality. They mould their lives, attitudes, thoughts and emotions on truth. They are truthful in belief, word, deed and thought. They trust in themselves. They are sincere, honest, humble and self-effacing.

They are courageous and fearless and proclaim truth, equality, love and justice. They never compromise with evil and oppression. They love knowledge and wisdom, and hate superstition. They do not fear any pharaoh, any god, idol, chief, lord and priest.

These moral qualities of truth, sincerity, humility, mutual trust and collective solidarity make the believers equal. They are equal since they share wealth and natural resources in common. Whatever talents, possessions, abilities, and merits they have they use them for collective well-being. They care for others. They have no selffish desires, no acquisitive motives. They do not exploit others' weaknesses, needs, labour and talents for their own aggrandizements.

In this Brotherhood of Truth superior are those who inclucate in them these virtues and qualities. These virtues are real as they emanate from the Divine source and are based on Divine goodness, power, mercy, wisdom and knowledge, and are revealed to the prophet-revolutionary who guides mankind on the straight path of truth and social equality.

Truth is revealed to the prophet-revolutionary in order to guide and enlighten the suffering humanity. He liberates them from the crushing bondage of oppression, inequality, superstition and darkness. But what is truth, according to the Qur'an? The next chapter answers this question with reference to the teachings of the Qur'an.

6

WHAT IS TRUTH?

According to the Qur'an, God is Truth and Reality. (20 : 114); 22 : 6, 62; 23 : 116; 31 : 30). The prophet-revolutionary is a man of God; and therefore a man of truth. Truth is constancy, faithfulness and agreement with God's will and plan. The prophet-revolutionay faithfully conforms his conduct, belief, ideas and thoughts to truth. He speaks the truth, thinks the truth and practises the truth. What he believes, says or does is all truth. Truth is a way of life. "It is He who has sent His apostle (Muhammad) with guidance and the way of truth that he may proclaim it over all other ways even though those who take partners with God may detest it," so says the Qur'an about the truth proclaimed by prophet Muhammad. (61: 9). And truth was the way of life of all prophet-revolutionaries, being the divinely inspired human beings.

1. Truth and Falsehood:

Opposite of truth is falsehood. Falsehood is something unreal, deceptive, unfaithful or fake. It is artificial, unnatural, not conforming to the will or plan of God. It is the way of untruth or error. It is the way of those who reject truth and soical equality and deny goodness, brotherhood and justice.

But what is the nature of truth and falsehood in relation to communities or societies of human beings? Truth may relate to an individual when he dedicates himself wholeheartedly to the cause of truth. Truth may be social or collective when a group of individuals believe in truth and establish a community based on the principle of truth. . . . . "Those who reject (God, truth) follow falsehood, while those who believe (in God, truth) follow the truth from their Lord". . . (47: 3).

The prophet-revolutionary brings truth to his contemporary society which in general, is deceived by falsehood and it runs after false appearances, glitter and glamour of worldly life. Those who follow untruth and false ways of corrupt life consider the prophet-revolutionary a madam, a liar, poet or a romantic-idealist who, for them, lives in a fool's paradise because he rejects selfishness, love of goods and chattels, greed, lust and dishonesty of the crowd. "Or do they not recognize their Apostle, that they deny him? Or do they say, 'He is possessed'? Nay, he has brought them the truth (*Haqq*) but most of them hate the truth. If the truth had conformed to their (false) desires, truly the heavens and the earth, and all beings therein would have been corrupted, Nay, We have sent them their admonition, but they turn away from their admonition." (23: 69–71).

The prophet-revolutionaries fight for truth; and truth is the cause of God because God is truth. "Those who believe (in God, truth) fight in the cause of God and those who reject (truth) fight in the cause of evil. So fight against the friends of Satan; feeble indeed is the stratagem of Satan." (4: 76).

As an individual may lie so a group of individuals may lie and perpetuate falsehood. A group of oppressors who persecute and exploit people at large is dishonest, false, corrupt and iniquitous. So sin is individual as well as social. The communities of oppressors, *Qura Zalima* represent falsehood. Their oppression and exploitation of the weak is a lie and a deception.

The prophet-revolutionaries fight for the cause of truth; and truth takes various forms in different socio-economic formations. To emancipate slaves, widows and orphans was a social truth in the pre-capitalist ancient societies. To liberate poor and weak working classes in a feudal/capitalist formation is also truth. Truth is thus a collective and social truth. A collective truth is the truth when a community believes in truth, social equality, love and brotherhood and struggles to establish a social order based on these social principles. Every thought, idea or act which assists in the emancipation of the weak is truth and righteousness.

Every policy and plan which helps in building an equalitarian society is an act of righteousness. . . ."Nothing could they (believers in truth and equality) suffer or do, but was reckoned to their credit as a deed of righteousness–whether they suffered thirst, or fatigue or hunger, in the cause of God, or trod paths to raise the ire of the rejecters (of truth, God), or received any injury whatever from an enemy; for God suffereth not the reward to be lost of those who do good;– nor could they spend anything (for the cause)– small or great– nor cut across a valley but the deed is inscribed to their credit; that God might requite their deed with the best (possible reward)." (9: 120–121).

According to the Qur'an, truth is conformity to the Divine will or nature. This means that its opposite untruth or falsehood is negation of Divine will or nature. All the things in nature willy nilly follow natural laws of harmony and conformity. Human nature in its Divine image inherently conforms to nature when man speaks the truth, follows his clean conscience like an innocent child whose interior and exterior are the same, who does not hide anything with base motive, does not fear or favour any person. He is faithfull and sincere to his pure nature. The moral and social values of honesty, sincerity, love and equality are values of truth because they make social life harmonious, peaceful, pure and rich.

On the other land, selfish desires, lust, greed, covetousness, jealousy, hatred, oppression and pride are unnatural and artificial values which are disharmonious and harmful for a healthy and balanced social life.

These are all false values which distort human nature, deaden the mind and harden the heart, as famine and draught destroy the fertility of a soil where nothing grows. Similarly evil and corruption, iniquity and injustice destroy the equilibrium and harmony of a social order by creating social classes on the basis of wealth, status, social origin, power and privileges. Equality and brotherhood are truth whereas inequallity and class division are falsehood.

Those who believe in truth and social equality and fight for this cause are, according to the Qur'an, really righteous–the people of truth. There are certain moral qualities of these people of truth which can take different social and moral characteristies in different societies. They firmly believe in truth, share their wealth and possessions with the poor, speak the truth, fulfil their promises and pledges and are always patient in adversities and persevere in difficulties, struggles and wars. "It is not righteousness that ye turn your faces towards East or West;

> "But it is righteousness to believe in God (truth) and the Last Day, and the Angels, and the Book and

> the Messengers; to spend of your wealth out of love for Him for your kin, for orphans, for the needy, for the wayfarer, for the poor and for emancipating slaves, to be steadfast in prayer and practise regular charity, to fulfil the contracts which ye have made; and to be firm and patient in pain (or suffering) and adversity, and throughout all periods of panic. *Such are the people of truth, the God-fearing."* (2: 177).

The life of a prophet-revolutionary is a constant struggle against evil and falsehood and against the communities of oppressors. The prophet-revolutionaries preach the truth and do not lose heart in the presence of evil: "We only send the apostles to give glad tidings and to give warnings. But those who reject (truth) dispute with the (help of) falsehood, in order therewith to weaken the truth, and they treat My Signs as a jest, as also the fact that they are warned! (18: 56).

Whenever truth struggles against falsehood and 'Message of God' comes, the powerful rich classes, the oppressors of the weak use all their wealth, manpower, resources and forces to crush truth and its message of social equality and brotherhood. They reject the message of truth and equality because it challenges their falsehood (*batil*), their power, wealth, arrogance and tyranny. "Never did We send a warner (a prophet-revolutionary) to a population but the wealthy ones among them said:

> We believe not in the (Message of truth and social equality) with which you have been sent. And they said: We have more in wealth and in sons, and we cannot be punished. Say: verily my Lord enlarges and restricts the provision to whom He pleases, but most men understand not. And it is not your wealth nor your sons, that will bring you nearer

to Us in degree: But only those who believe (in truth) and work righteousness—these are the ones for whom there is a multiplied reward for their deeds, while secure they (reside) in the dwellings on high.!" (34: 34–37).

2. Representation and Explanation of Truth By Parables.

Truth is plain, modest, frank, artless and unassuming, unpretentious, candid and guileless. It is bright and clear like the shining Sun; it is beautiful and fragrant like the smell of a flower. It is naturally flowing like a calm and quiet river. It is still and tranquil like the heart of a 'man of God. Truth is innocence, humility, simplicity and sincerity. One who is sincere is clean, pure, unmixed, and unfeigned, and genuine. Sincerity is the same within as without. It is selflessness. It is patience, perseverance and constancy. It is natural and spontaneous, open, courageous and bold, fearless and resolute. Truth does not pretend, nor does it deceive, cheat or mislead. Truth is clarity and perspicuity, purity and chastity. Truth is wisdom. Truth is knowledge. Truth is power. Truth does not lie. It does not simulate and pretend. It is the same without what it is within. There is no difference. Truth is not a deception or a falsehood. It appears what it is in reality.

Truth is conformity to reality; it is faithfulness and adherence to nature, or in the words of the Qur'an, it is a total, sincere, unalloyed submission to the universal will and plan of God Who is all truth, power, knowledge and wisdom. Truth is justice, love, equality and brotherhood. Truth is humility.

Truth is expressed through words, concepts, ideas, idioms, languages, through sense perceptions and mental images. Religious literature has throughout the ages used parables to articulate, express and explain in simple terms the complex problems of society, nature, history, revelation, revolution, human destiny and the eternal conflict between goodness and evil.

A parable in the Qur'an is a simple story, similitude, narrative, fable or an example which illustrates some social problem in order to bring out the inherent moral significance of the issue. Its basic aim is to make the problem clear, simple, perceptible and understandable to the common people who have not attained intellectual refinements and sophistications but who are simple and uncorrupted by false desires and deceptive appearances, and selfish motives and impulses.

The Qur'an is replete with simple parables which expressed in the contemporary idiom and language convey the Quranic message of truth and social equality to the contemporary people in a highly impressive, forceful and pithy diction and style.

At a time when natural and social sciences and their scientific methodology of discovering new knowledge and truth were not available to the common people, parables, and similes were generally used by the prophets, wisemen, sages and sagacious leaders to represent and explain truth and principles and rules which governed societies and communities, their origins, growth and decline. The contrasts between goodness and evil, truth and falsehood and conflicts between the forces of right and wrong, between God and Satan are also allegorical.

The Qur'an explains the truth of revelation with parables. Hypocrisy, deception, pride, jealousy and oppression are like darkness, and truth, humility, sincerity, justice and equality are like light. The first parable of the Qur'an (2: 17–18) is about the nature of truth and falsehood. The similitude of those who reject truth and honesty "is that of a man who kindled a fire, when it lighted all around him God took away their light and left them in utter darkness so they could not see. Deaf, dumb, and blind, they will not return (to the path of truth)".

Truth is an everlasting light and a constant brilliance which brightens the path of the man of truth. Truth is not ephemeral or temporary. Lie and deception are temporary things, an unreal and false show. Power of wealth, lands, gold and silver, arrogance, oppression, jealousy, and compromise with evil and the corrupt, or hypocrisy may succeed for a time and win temporary success and fame, 'like the man in the darkness who kindled a fire.'

But there is no real light of truth and sincerity, there is no faith, nor belief in one's cause. Therefore such a deficient light will mislead the ignorant and superstitious to a pit of death and darkness. In confusion and darkness they cannot help each other; they are groping in the dark like dumb, deaf and blind people who cannot see, hear or speak; they are like animals or even worse than animals. So the light is truth and darkness is untruth.

The problems of the Qur'an are from ordinary human life, from nature, from the flesh and blood of living human beings, pertaining to their real life, its problems, ideals, aspirations, emotions, victories and defeats, virtues and vices, human weaknesses, corruption and evil, goodness and righteousness. These similes and parables are taken from natural phenomenon, from rain, rivers, clouds, mountains, tempests, oceans, plants, trees and animals, from everything which happens around human beings, from past history and from the rise and fall of human societies and civilizations.

The parable of the light and darkness shows that truth is always simple, straightforward, spontaneous and candid like an eternal light which guides and shows the right path. On the other hand, untruth is falsehood, it is completely treacherous, deceptive, with intrigues and stratagems, embellished with hypocrisy, wrapped in layers and crusts of artificiality and false rationalizations. It is darkness in which all distinctions, marks and signs between what is right and what is wrong, are obliterated. Truth is direct and simple, clear and manifest, whereas falsehood is tortuous, opaque and obscure, dark and sinister.

The parables in the Qur'an are thus simple illustrations of truth with deeper social import. They explain, elucidate and simplify social and economic intricacies, riddles, contrasts, contradictions and complexities with direct references, and illustrations from natural life, even from the examples of flies, mosquitoes, spiders and camels which the common people can easily understand, appreciate and apply in their daily lives as higher moral values of truth, sincerity, honesty etc. "God disdains not to use the similitude of things lowest as well as highest," says the Qur'an; "those who believe know that it is truth from their Lord; but those who reject (God, truth) say, what means God by this similitude? By it He causes many to stray and many He leads into the right path; but He causes not to stray, except those who forsake (the path of truth)". (2: 26).

Hearts as hard as a stone:

Describing the backsliding of the Israelites after their covenant, pledging that they would abide by truth, social equality, and sincerity, the Qur'an compares the hearts of those who rejected truth to the hardness of stones. Even stones are not so hard as the hearts of the habitual liars and oppressors: "Thenceforth your hearts hardened: they became like a rock and even worse in hardness. For among rocks there are some from which rivers gush forth: others there are which when split asunder send forth water; and others which sink for fear of God. And God is not unmindful of what ye do" (2: 74).

The Dumb Driven Cattle:

Those who reject truth and follow untruth, inequality, jealousy, pride, selfishness, oppression and injustice are like the 'dumb driven cattle,' who are senseless, callous and wild and who cannot distinguish between right and wrong, true and false as they have no sense or perception of higher moral values. "The parable of those who reject (truth) is as if one were to shout like a goat-herd, to things that listen to nothing but calls and cries: deaf, dumb and blind, they are void of wisdom." (2: 171).

Spider's Web:

An iniquitous social order, in which the powerful rich classes oppress and misguide the weak and poor classes, is unstable like a spider's web. A violent storm, or even a strong wind tends to destroy the flimsy threads and weak structures of the web. The Qur'an compares such oppressive communities, *Qura Zalima,* to spider's web:

> And (We destroyed) Qarun, Pharaoh, and Haman: there came to them Moses with Clear Signs, but they behaved with insolence on the earth: Yet they could not overreach (Us). Each one of them We seized for

> his crime: of them, against some We sent a violent tornado; some were caught by a Blast; some We caused the earth to swallow up; and some We drowned (in the waters): It was not God who oppressed them: they oppressed their own selves. The parable of those who take protectors other than God is that of the spider, who builds (to itself) a house; but truly the flimsiest of houses is the spider's house, if they but knew. Verily God doth know of (every thing) whatever that they call upon besides Him: and He is Exalted (in Power), Wise. And such are the parables We set for mankind, but only those understand them who have knowledge.(29: 39–43).

Such parables are simple and of common occurrence visible to all who can see and ponder over their nature and character. Their moral and social significance can only be understood by those who have knowledge and pursue truth. The corrupt social orders in which the powerful classes oppress and enslave the lower classes are weak and unstable because the arrogant rich not only weaken the poor masses and mislead and confuse them, but they also enfeeble themselves through arrogance, selfishness, corruption, false pride, vanities and self-sufficiency which ultimately ruin them. Self-complacency is self-delusion.

Qarun, Pharaoh and Haman are the symbolic characters and representatives of the powerful oppressors who had through their iniquitous institutions and deceptive ideologies and religions enslaved the poor people. The prophet-revolutionary revolted against this community of the oppressors, destroyed them and emancipated the slaves. Musa (Moses) represented the forces of truth and equality, and Pharaoh, Qarun and Haman led the oppressors. Truth ultimately triumphs over untruth and falsehood.

The Qur'an illustrates truth and falsehood, justice and iniquity with the examples of a good tree and a bad tree. Truth and justice ensure stability, security and strength, but falsehood and oppression lead to weakness and destruction. The ruling rich classes exploit the lower classes and drive them to social ruin, economic deprivation and moral depravity since an oppressive social order has no roots:

> "Seest thou not how God sets forth a parable?— a goodly word (deed) like a goodly tree, whose root is firmly fixed, and its branches (reach) to the heavens, it brings forth its fruit at all times, by the leave of its Lord. So God sets forth parables for men, in order that they may receive admonition. And the parable of an evil word (deed) is that of an evil tree. It is torn up by the root from the surface of the earth. It has no stability. God will establish in strength those who believe (in truth) with the word (or thing) that stands firm in this world and in the Hereafter; but doeth what He willeth". (14: 24–27).

Truth is like a good tree in its beauty, fruitfulness, stability, and firmness. It stands upright and is never shaken by storms of calamities, or temporary shocks or defeats. The roots of truth go deeper in the real facts, problems and relations of life. Its fruits spread all around, its branches sprout upwards to absorb sunshine and inspiration from natural and divine sources. Its fruits are the enjoyment of its blessing, its benefits reach all; it betters and reforms life. The man of truth who dedicates his life for propagation of truth is sincere, selfless and humble. Like the fruit tree, the life of the man of truth is a constant source of sweetness, love, solace, sympathy and goodness for others.

The evil tree or falsehood is unstable; it has no roots and no firm foundation. It is the source of all lies, deceptions, fraud and corruption. It spreads iniquity, cruelty, greed, pride, ignorance and superstition. Such is oppression (*Zulm*) which has no base. The oppressors drive the weak classes to chaos, confusion and perdition. "Hast thou not turned thy vision to those who have changed the favour of God into denial (of truth) and caused their people to descend to the House of perdition." (14: 28).

Truth Everlasting:

The man of truth is always humble and sincere, he never boasts of his knowledge, power, truth, position, influence or of any worldy possession. He is self-effacing, selfless, ever seeking to improve himself. He is intensely conscious of his shortcomings and weaknesses. The man of falsehood, on the other hand, runs after false appearances; he is puffed up with what he possesses. He accumulates material goods of comforts and ease, show and ostentation. He is proud of his wealth, knowledge, sons and power. He forgets higher moral values. The worldly possessions, material powers and strength are ephemeral while truth is everlasting. At the end, the man of truth will be saved and the man of falsehood and his worldly wealth and power will be destroyed.

What is true of an individual is also true of classes and nations. A corrupt society and a depraved nation are destroyed but a righteous, educated, truthful and egalitarian just society prospers: "Tell them the parable of two men," says the Qur'an, "for one of them We provided two gardens of grape-vines and surrounded them with date-palms; and between the two We placed corn fields. Each of those gardens brought forth its produce

> and failed not in the least therein: in the midst of them We caused a river to flow: (Abundant) was the produce this man had: he said to his companion, in the course of a mutual argument: 'More wealth have I than you and more honour and power in (my following of) men'. He went into his garden in a state (of mind) unjust to his soul: He said, 'I deem not that this will ever perish, nor do I deem that the Hour (of Judgement) will (ever) come. Even if I am brought back to my Lord, I shall surely find (there) something better in exchange. His companion said to him in the course of the argument with him:' Dost thou deny Him who created thee from dust, then out of a sperm-drop then fashioned thee into a man? But (I think) for my part that He is God (Truth), my Lord, and none shall I associate with my Lord. Why didst thou not, as thou wentest into thy garden, say: 'God's will (be done), there is no power but with God, if thou dost see me less than thee in wealth and sons, it may be that my Lord will give me something better than thy garden, and that He will send on thy garden thunderbolts (by way of reckoning) from heaven, making it (but) slippery sand! Or the water of the garden will run off underground so that thou wilt never be able to find it.
>
> So his fruits (and enjoyment) were encompassed (with ruin) and he remained twisting and turning his hands over what he had spent on his property, which had (now) tumbled to pieces to its very foundations, and he could only say: Woe is me! Would I had never ascribed partners to my Lord and Cheri-

sher. Nor had he any people to help him against God, nor was he able to deliver himself. There the (only) protection comes from God, the True One. He is the Best to reward, and the Best to give success." (18: 32–44).

The man who was proud of his material wealth and possessions insolently relied on his economic power and people but nothing could help him. He was ruined and his attitude of mind, thought and ideas which were built around his insolence and a selfish sense of self-sufficiency removed him away from the source of higher values, truth, justice and equality. He was not only cruel to his fellows but also to himself. On the other hand, the man of truth, though less affluent than the former, was a humble and contented man who believed in truth and spurned material goods, offices and worldly possessions which are for him insignificant and unsubstantial things.

Truth Prevails:

Falsehood may flourish for a while which is a test for the patience, constancy and perseverance of those who chart for themselves a course of truth and rectitude, goodness and justice. The life of falsehood, of deception and illustion, superstition and darkness, the life spent in collecting material goods of this life and in running after wealth, power and self glory is compared by the Qur'an to a sudden shower or gust of rain:

"Tell them the similitude of the life of this world: it is like the rain which We send down from the skies. The earth's vegetation absorbs it, but soon it becomes dry stubble, which the winds do scatter; it is (only) God who prevails over all things. Wealth and sons are allurements of the life of the world, but the things that endure, good deeds, are best in the sight of thy Lord, as rewards, and best as (the foundation for) hopes." (18: 45–46).

Only good deeds, truth, honesty, sincerity, social equality, justice, love and brotherhood will prevail in the end.

Truth is Light:

"God is Truth–High above all." (20: 114) "God is the light of the heavens and the earth. The parable of His light is as if there were a Niche and within it a lamp, the lamp enclosed in glass; the glass as it were a brilliant star lit from a blessed tree, an olive, neither of the east nor of the west whose oil is well-nigh luminous, though fire scarce touched it. Light upon light! God doth guide whom He will to His light. God doth set forth parables for men: and God doth know all things." (24: 35).

Niche represents habitation or source of truth which is open to human beings by a special way, 'yet closed to those who refuse its rays'. The lamp is the truth, the real light and illumination. The glass represents the transparent medium through which the light is reflected.

Truth is expressed through human language or perceived through human mind and then made intelligible to mankind at large in human forms, modes and methods. The men of truth who love mankind and proclaim social equality and brotherhood reflect this light and spread it to the world when they build actual social orders based on these higher principles.

On the contrary are those who deny truth, social equality and brotherhood. "Their deeds are like a mirage in sandy deserts, which the man parched with thirst mistakes for water until when he comes upto it he finds it to be nothing. But he finds God (ever) with him, and

God will pay him his account; and God is swift in taking account. Or their state is like the depths of darkness in vast deep ocean, overwhelmed with billow topped by billow, topped by (dark) clouds: depths of darkness one above another. If a man stretches out his hand, he can hardly see it! For any to whom God giveth no light, there is no light." (24: 39–40).

Those who lead the lives of untruth live in darkness. Untruth is deception and illusion. The man of falsehood follows false desires, false passions and false goals. Like a thirsty man who is deceived by a mirage in the desert he dies in the agony of thirst, since all his life he chased unreal things and empty shadows.

The man who cuts himself from the light of truth falls in the pit of darkness. According to the Qur'an, the prophet-revolutionary is a man of truth who brings human beings from darkness to light. The true scholars and revolutionaries of modern times are also people of truth who discover knowledge and enlighten mankind and struggle for social equality, love and brotherhood. Revolution and scholarship must fight for the cause of truth as revolution and scholarship are nothing but discovery and supremacy of truth.

Truth is knowledge. Truth is justice, equality and freedom. Those scholars who pursue their selfish interests and conceal evidence in order to subdue truth and thus help oppressors and evil-doers lead humanity to darkness and ruin. Their obfuscation of truth and knowledge is harmful for mankind, because ignorance and misguidance bring confusion, chaos and ultimate defeat and death to nations. Mentioning the misguided scholars and priests, the Qur'an says: "The similitude of those who were charged with the (obligations of the) Mosaic law, but who subsequently failed in those (obligations) is that of an ass which carries huge tomes (but understands them not). Worst is the similitude of people who falsify the Signs of God and God guides not people who oppress (the weak)". (62: 5).

And 'Signs of God' are the laws, principles, tendencies which govern this universe, man, his society, history and all the natural phenomena. These 'Signs of God' or principles, behind social and natural phenomena are discovered by those who follow truth and are sincere, humble, selfless, like the prophet-revolutionaries of the ancient times.

3. The Parable of Fruit-Garden as a Socio-economic Order:

Any socio-economic order, primitive, tribal, feudal or pre-feudal–in its various aspects–is simplified and compared by the Qur'an to a fruit– garden. The fruit grows due to the work of different classes of people: labourers, sowers, reapers, gleaners, artisans, blacksmiths, carpenters, potters, cobblers, masons and others who directly or indirectly participate in producing the crop. They all constitute the social structure of the economy of an eastern village where the menial labouring classes, as in Arabia, have been considered by the powerful land-owners, merchants and priests as inferior and abominable subjects fit for oppression and suppression. The workers are taken as animals or beasts of burden.

But by custom they are entitled to their due share in the crop when it is harvested as they form an important and useful part of the village community. If the rich owners, through deceit and intrigue, deprive these poor labourers of their legitimate share this would weaken the entire social structure. Such unjust social orders which deprive the working classes of their rights and shares never survive. This is the theme of the parable of the garden. (68: 17–33). This parable underlines the principle that without social and economic justice no social equality is guaranteed and without it no society is stable and strong.

The Qur'an tells the prophet that he should not hearken to those rich and powerful people who deny (Truth) and offered him impossible compromises. The man of truth never compromises on his principles of truth, justice and social equality for which he fights against the oppressors of the weak people: " So hearken not to those who deny (the Truth): their desire is that thou shouldst be pliant, so would they be pliant. Heed not the type of despicable (rich) man–ready with oaths, a slanderer, going about with calumnies, (habitually) hindering (all) good, transgressing beyond bounds, deep in sin; violent (and cruel), with all that, base-born, because he possesses wealth and (numerous) sons. When to him are rehearsed Our Signs, 'Tales of the Ancient', he cries. Soon shall We brand (the beast) on the snout; verily We have tried them as We tried the people of the Garden when they resolved to gather the fruits of the

> (garden) in the morning but made no reservation (If it be God's Will"). So there came on the (garden) a visitation from thy Lord, (which swept away) all around, while they were asleep. So the (garden) became, by the morning, like a dark and desolate spot (whose fruit had been gathered). As the morning broke, they called out, one to another 'go ye to your tilth in the morning, if ye would gather the fruits.' So they departed conversing in secret low tones, (saying), let not a single poor person break in upon you into the (garden) this day'. And they opened the morning, strong in an (unjust)

> resolve, but when they saw the (garden), they said: 'We have surely lost our way. Indeed we are shut out (of the fruits of our labour).. Said one of them more just (than the rest); 'did I not say to you, why not glorify (God)?' They said: Glory to our Lord'! Verily we have been oppressors (of the weak). Then they turned, one against another, in reproach. They said: Alas for us! We have indeed transgressed! It may be that our Lord will give us in exchange a better (garden) than this: for we do turn to Him (in repentance). Such is the punishment (in this life); but greater is the punishment in the Hereafter, if only they knew." (68: 8–33).

The owners of the garden were rich men who were proud, selfish and oppressive for the poor workers. Under the cover of darkness they conspired to deprive the poor workers of their shares in the crop. As a result, the deprived workers became the cause of the destruction of the garden. Pride goeth before a fall.

This parable shows that the rich owners of the orchard conspired to steal away the rightful shares of the poor workers. Their selfish motive and acquisitive impulse hardened their hearts and deceived their minds and drove them to exploit them. This greed became the cause of their ruin. They wanted to cheat them through deception, trickery, and cunning to show to the wide world that they were not aware of the rights and shares of the poor workers.

They tried to crush the poor but in the vicious circle of their greed, covetousness and fraud they weakened the whole social order and ultimately destroyed it making it a desolate wilderness where no capital remained, no fruit-tree survived, no gain and profit accrued; that is, all the economic and social institutions, relations and privileges were disrupted.

The Slave of Many Masters:

The unregenerate man who leads a life of falsehood, greed, cruelty, hypocrisy and superstition is without any stable centre of truth, constancy and faithfulness. He is like a slave who tries to serve and please many masters but stumbles and falls down. He has no will of his own. He sells his soul and thus loses his freedom to act.

A person who denies truth runs from pillar to post, from one selfish desire to another, from one god to another god, from a lower economic status to a higher one through hook or crook, and assembles goods upon goods. He wavers, trembles and succumbs to the idol of Mammon, to perdition and ruin. "God puts forth a parable: a man belonging to many partners at variance with each other: and a man belonging entirely to one master. Are those two equal in comparison?" (39: 29). "Who, then, doth more wrong than one who utters a lie concerning God and rejects the truth when it comes to him? Is there not in Hell an abode for those who deny (truth)? And he who brings the truth and he who confirms (and supports) it–such are those who do right. They shall have all that they wish for in the presence of their Lord: such is the reward of those who do good. So that God will turn off from them (even) the worst in their deeds and give them their reward according to the best of what they have done." (39: 32–35).

This parable explains the difference between those who follow truth and conform their lives, deeds, thoughts and ideas to it, and those who lead false lives of base desires, felfish motives, corruption and fraud and run after fleeting shadows. Those who follow truth and act righteously by ameliorating the lot of the poor, "they shall have all that they wish for" and shall accomplish the impossible tasks of bringing equality, justice and prosperity to all—those who are truthful and sincere. They shall gain real freedom and brotherhood, mutual trust, faith and solidarity. But those who are insincere and false and reject truth and equality lose their natural freedom and fall into the slavery of many idols of wealth, of human flesh, of power, desire, lust, superstition, influence and status and of many human gods.

They belong to many masters who themselves have divergent aims. The slave tries to serve so many masters at the cost of his self-respect, honour, dignity and freedom. He dies morally since death is not physical only; they also die who kill their consciences, harden their hearts and follow their baser instincts and wild emotions.

Such a person, in another parable, is compared by the Qur'an to a useless thing without weight and significance: "As if he had fallen from the sky and been snatched up by birds, or the wind has swooped (like a bird on its prey) and thrown him into a far distant place." (22:31).

The man who denies truth and obeys beings, gods and powers, rulers and tyrants other than One True God, is like the man who falls from the sky and does not have any thing to grasp and rely on. He is hurled by his passions, swayed by his desires and tossed by his fancies like a light and thin object. He has no aim and no purpose except his animal desires and instincts.

The Firm Rock and the undermined Sand-Cliff:

A man who builds his life on truth, sincerity and social equality, stands on a firm rock that will never break. He strives hard to oppose oppression of all sorts. He is against exploitation of the poor by the rich based on social and economic injustices, and against deceptions and frauds of all kinds, superstition and ignorance. On the other hand, an oppressor who denies truth (and hence God) is the man who builds on a shifting sand-cliff on the brink of an abyss which has no firm ground. This edifice of an unjust order will collapse, so says the Qur'an:

> "Which then is best?– he that layeth his foundation on piety to God and His Good Pleasure?– or he that layeth his foundation on an undermined sand-cliff ready to crumble to pieces? And it doth crumble to pieces with him into the fire of Hell. And God guideth not people that oppress. The foundation of those who so build is never free from suspicion and shakiness in their hearts until their hearts are cut to pieces. And God is All-Knowing, Wise." (9: 109–110).

The man who is not true, sincere and honest has no security, stability and surety. As he has no central basis and purpose he is shaken by fears, suspicions, doubts and superstitions. He has no patience, constancy and integrity as he runs from one point to another, from one false desire to another, and at last falls a prey to them. His passions control him and his false desires put him in a prison of darkness, pain and superstition from which he has no escape.

Man of Truth is a Free and Courageous Person:

A true man of God is a just person, and a just person is a free person, free from baser desires, lusts, passions and superstitions. He tells the truth, he believes in human equality and brotherhood, human freedom and integrity.

A man who deviates from truth is like a dumb slave who obeys many idols and serves false gods: "God sets forth the parable of two men: one of them dumb with no power of any sort; a wearisome burden is he to his master, whichever way he directs him, he brings no good. Is such a person equal with one who commands justice and is on a straight path?" (16: 76).

Another parable is that of a slave "who is under the dominion (of a free person). He has no power of any sort; and (the other) a man on whom We have bestowed goodly favour from Ourselves, and he spends thereof (freely) secretly and openly. Are the two equal?" (16: 75).

The Qur'an compares the man of God (i.e. one who strives for the cause of truth and equality with his life, labour and possessions) to the man of evil (who deviates from truth and pursues injustice and oppression of the poor) to the fertile garden and the barren rock:

> "O ye who believe render not vain the spending of your possessions by ostentatious hypocrisy and harm, like him who spends his possessions only to be seen of men and does not believe in God and the Last Day. His simile is the simile of a rock on which is dust, a rainstorm strikes it leaving it bare. Such people have no power over what they have gained. God does not guide the people who deny (truth)."
>
> And the example of those who spend their possessions in search of God's pleasure and for the strengthening of their souls is like the example of a garden on a height. Heavy rain falls on it and it brings forth its fruit two-fold. And if heavy rain does not fall on it then dew-drops (are enough). God is seer of what ye do". (2: 264–265).

This parable has deeper social significance. The prophet-revolutionaries who build a social order on the higher values of truth, social equality and brotherhood spend their substance; i.e. plan their social economy in its distribution and consumption aspects to promote general welfare, economic equality and justice. There are no oppressors and oppressed, rich and poor, but all are equal. The goal of political economy is a regimen of justice, equality and truth. This is a classless society: Social equality ensures stability and justice and brotherhood guarantee prosperity and solidarity.

Cause of God is the cause of truth, equality, love and brotherhood. A just and egalitarian society safeguards the rights of all its members: no weak individual, group or class is exploited by the more powerful and wealthy. "The parable of those who spend their substance in the way of God is that of a grain of corn: it groweth seven ears, and each ear hath a hundred grains. God giveth manifold increase to whom He pleaseth. And God careth for all and he knoweth all things". (2: 261).

Truth was exemplified and illustrated by the prophet-revolutionaries in their hard struggies against the forces of evil. What they said and believed they acted upon it. Their lives were demonstrations and proofs of the truth revealed to them. They were human beings and therefore ideal models for emulation. They were men of God and could become kings and leaders of their people. They could amass mountains of gold and silver and could live in lofty mansions and palaces. But they gave up all for the sake of their cause. They were interested in higher values, principles and ideals of life; and material and transitory things did not matter for them.

They forsook material possessions because God does not come to the heart of a man which has become as hard as gold. Men of God renounce material goods and worldly possessions to have the spiritual light of God. They had to suffer like ordinary human beings; therefore they lived amidst suffering human beings and shared their joys and pains. They showed them the way of courage, patience and perseverance. They led them to the paradise of truth, social equality, love and brotherhood.

The next part discusses the lives and characters of these men of God, the paragons of excellence, beauty, truth, knowledge and wisdom, freedom and human dignity. They showed the spiritual, moral and intellectual heights to which man can rise.

7

ADAM – THE FIRST PROPHET WHO FOUGHT AGAINST IGNORANCE AND EVIL.

1. The Prophet-revolutionaries in the Qur'an:

According to the Qur'an, all creatures in the universe willy-nilly have to abide by the Will and Plan of God. This is the natural-universal covenant and law of every existing thing. The Prophet-revolutionaries bear responsibilities higher than those of other human and natural beings. They have solemnly pledged and entered into a covenant that they shall carry out their mission, courageously proclaim the truth they have and shall always, under all circumstances, in war and in peace, in adversity and in prosperity comply by this covenant. This is a solemn pledge for which they are responsible. They must guide people to the right path of truth and sincerity and build a society on these higher values:

> "And remember We took from the prophets their Covenant as (We did) from thee (O Muhammad!): from Nuh, Ibrahim, Musa and 'Isa, the son of Maryam: We took from them a solemn Covenant: that (God) may question the (custodians) of truth concerning the truth (they were charged with) and He has prepared for the Unbelievers a grievous penalty." (33: 7–8).

The prophets were human beings made of flesh and

blood as all human beings are. They had families, wives and children, parents and relations. They lived and worked among the common people sharing their joys and sorrows, pains and sufferings. They lived amidst ordinary people, tolerated their petty, narrow and superstitious behaviour and acted as models of high moral character. They taught them by example and practice. They did not mince words and sermonize but whatever they taught they first acted upon it themselves. They were divinely-inspired teachers and leaders of the common people.

They were divinely charged of the heavy responsibility of proclaiming truth. They were therefore men of truth, honesty and sincerity. They believed in human equality, and brotherhood of mankind. All were equal in their presence. They did not fear or favour powerful human beings because they obeyed and pleased One God only who is the source of all truth, power, wisdom, knowledge, justice, mercy, and goodness.

All prophet-revolutionareis have many common traits: they upheld truth and resolutely faced evil and falsehood; they revolted against the social order of tyranny and oppression which divided their societies into classes of masters and slaves, oppressors and oppressed. They founded and organized new communities of truth, equality and brotherhood. Only the lower classes of slaves, workers, women and orphans, and other weak and poor people believed in their message.

The powerful rulers always tried to tempt the prophet-revolutionaries with offers of wealth, power and position. Their intention was to neutralize the revolt of the proletariat. But the proletariat and their selfless beader never compromised. They were persecuted, exiled and even killed. Truth never compromises with falsehood and iniquity.

The revolutionareis and prophets who armed themselves and were able to defend their revolutions succeeded in liberating the oppressed masses but those who remained unarmed were defeated, crushed and destroyed, by their enemies. Therefore war for their defence (*Jihad*) became a necessary strategy for them.

All prophets were first considered liars, poets, idealists, soothsayers, sorcerers and agents of foreign enemies because these rebels threatened the entrenched corrupt social orders and tended to destroy all false ideologies, superstitions, cults, rituals and misconceptions about man, society and the universe.

These prophet-revolutionaries were sent to every community in all times. They were guided and inspired by God to lead the suffering humanity. The Qur'an records only those prophets who appeared in the Near East. They liberated the oppressed and slaves and tried to establish new communities based on the principles of truth, equality, justice, freedom and brotherhood.

Adam, Nuh, Hud, Salih, Ibrahim, Yusuf, Da'ud, Shu'ayb, Musa, 'Isa, Muhammad and many others were all righteous men. They proclaimed truth and equality and waged relentless war against evil and oppression. Almost all of them had to migrate to new abodes from where they initiated their struggle against the social orders of iniquity.

They were prophets and revolutionaries who revolted against the unjust orders. They were men of courage, forbearance, patience, wisdom and humility. They gave new criteria of judging right from wrong and good from bad. For them, every act and thought which promoted truth, equality and justice and combated evil and oppression, was a righteous act; and everything which aided oppression and exploitation of the poor and weak was evil, wrong-doing, falsehood and *Kufr*. *Kafir* is a person who denies truth and equality and exploits the poor. He is an enemy of truth and adversary of God and all goodness.

The Qur'an is the divine book which essentially narrates in parables and similes, the hard struggle of the prophet-revolutionaries against the forces of evil, oppression, exploitation, selfishness, greed, lust and pride. It is a declaration of war against those who reject truth and equality. The struggle of Muhammad against the overlords and slave-owners of Arabia, is actually the struggle of all prophet-revolutionaries against the oppressors of all sorts.

Whenever the prophets proclaimed their message of truth the rich rulers rejected it: they used to consider the humble leader of the poor people a powerless and weak human being whom only the lowly followed and who himself lived like an ordinary poor man since he identified himself with the humble and the lowly:

> "And the Chiefs of his (prophet's) people who rejected (truth) and denied the Meeting in the Hereafter, and on whom We had hestowed wealth and riches of this life, said: 'He is no more than a man like yourselves, he eats of that of which ye eat, and drinks of what ye drink. If ye obey a man like yourselves, behold it is certain ye will be lost." (23: 33–34).

Those who were living false lives of lust and greed aspired to follow powerful and rich chiefs who could apparently protect them from dangers and could bestow on them riches and favours. What a poor prophet could give them who had himself nothing to eat and nothing to wear? "He is only a man who invents a lie against God, but we are not the ones to believe in him" (23: 38).

"Then We sent Our apostles in succession," says the Qur'an "every times there came to a people their apostle they accused him of falsehood. So we made them follow each other (in punishment). We made them as a tale (that is told). So away with a people that will not believe (in truth)." (23: 44).

The haughty people refused to recognize the prophets and believe in them. They called them mad and possessed. The prophets brought them the truth "but most of them hate the truth. If the truth had been in accord with their desires, truly the heavens and the earth, and all beings therein would have been corrupted." (23: 70–71).

The truth brought by the prophets was to lead and guide mankind on the right path of equality, love and brotherhood. They had to change the world and overthrow the social orders of the oppressors.

2. Adam, the Original Man:

Adam is the first original man, the father and founder of mankind. He is the first prophet, the vicegerent, *Wasiy* of God on earth, He is *Safiy Allah,* 'the chosen of God'. He was the first divinely-inspired man who received revelation, mercy, power, knowledge and wisdom from God. God infused in him something of His own Soul, Spirit or Breath. He could do whatever he wished if he acted according to the Divine will and plan and conformed to his original innocence and truth patterned in the Divine image.

The advent of Adam on this earth is the beginning of his struggle and toil amidst hostile natural forces which he must subdue and control. This is the beginning of strife, conflict and contradiction between Good and Evil. Adam is the original, natural, innocent, wise, and honest man who is tempted and lured by the onslaughts of evil, primeval darkness and ignorance symbolized as Satan or Iblis. Adam was in the 'paradise of bliss,' and on the Right Path of truth, wisdom and innocence, and Satan lurked around this Straight Path leading to God.

Satan was arrogant, insolent and jealous of the natural talents, spiritual powers and innate capabilities of man. Arrogance and jealousy threw Satan into the fiery state of rebellion. Evil thus tempts the innocent man who is already forewarned at his birth about evil, greed, lust and arrogance.

The story of man therefore starts with the very creation of Adam and his struggle against evil. This is, of course, metaphorical and allegorical in the nature of a simile or parable to explain mystery of man's origin, his will power and knowledge, and also his weak nature. This explanation of man's creation is not scientific in the biological sense. The allegory of Adam and Satan is a religious simplification of the eternal conflict between the forces of goodness and evil.

Created from dust and of lowly and humble origins, says the Qur'an, man is naturally a weak creation, always in danger of temptations and enticements from powerful forces of evil. But man ultimately rises higher and higher, above plant and animal life to the status of prophethood, to the position of nearness to God where he sees everything clearly revealed to his inward eye, and thus strengthened by Divine inspiration or 'Holy Spirit' he succeeds in subduing evil or the natural and dark forces within himself or in the external world.

He acquires supremacy over angelic and natural forces; that is, man is destined to become the master of himself, of nature, of universe, society and history. Through his wisdom, knowledge, power, and higher values and principles he can create a paradise on earth and control his destiny and develop his natural talents to the full. The following Quranic verses of the Sura Al-A'raf, the Heights, (7) typically portray Adam's advent on earth and his struggles, and his ascent towards moral and spiritual heights:

> "It is We who created you and gave you shape; then We bade the angels bow down to Adam and they bowed down; not so Iblis. He refused to be of those who bow down. (God) said,: 'What prevented thee from bowing down when I commanded thee? He said: 'I am better than he: Thou didst create me from fire and him from clay. God said: 'Get thee down from this; it is not for thee to be arrogant here, get out, for thou art of the meanest (of creatures).' He said: 'Give me respite till the day they are raised up'. (God) said: Be thou among those who have respite.' He said: 'Because thou hast thrown me out of the way, lo! I will lie in wait for them on Thy Straight Path. Then will I assault them from before them and behind them, from their right and their left. Nor wilt Thou find in most of them gratitude (for Thy mercies)'. God said: 'Get out from this, disgraced and expelled. If any of them follow thee, –Hell will I fill with you all'".
> (7: 11–18).

Then follows the eternal war between right and wrong, good and evil, humility and arrogance, love and jealousy. The opposition between good and evil was born with man. Man was innocent, natural, simple and righteous. Now he was tempted by evil. If man cannot subdue his evil passions of greed, lust, arrogance, jealousy and hatred he falls below the level of animals. If he can control himself and resist evil and follow the straight path of truth and innocence he can rise above his material and natural conditions even above angels, the natural powers. And he can subject all nature, history and society to his will. Prophecy of Adam was the prophecy of truth, enlightenment, and knowledge. The Straight Path is the path of God, the way of life of truth, justice and goodness. It is not the path of schism, disunity, iniquity, discord and division: "Verily, this is My way, leading straight: follow it; follow not (other) paths: they will scatter you about from His (great) Path. Thus doth He command you, that ye may be righteous." (6: 153).

And Adam was forewarned about the evil forces. The Qur'an says:

> "O Adam; dwell thou and thy wife in the Garden and enjoy (its good things) as ye wish: but approach not this tree or ye run into harm and transgression. Then began Ṣatan to whisper suggestions to them, bringing openly before their minds all their shame that was hidden from them (before): he said: your Lord only forbade you this tree, lest ye should become angels or such beings as live for ever. And he swore to them both, that he was their sincere adviser. So by deceit he brought about their fall: when they tasted of the tree their shame became manifest to them, and they began to sew together the leaves of the Garden over their bodies. And their Lord called unto them: 'Did I not forbid you that tree and tell you that Satan was an avowed enemy unto you'. They said: 'Our Lord: we have wronged our own souls; if thou forgive us not and bestow not upon us thy mercy, we shall certainly be lost. God said 'Get ye down, with enmity between yourselves, On earth will be your dwelling-place and your means of livelihood–for a time. He said: 'therein

shall ye live, and therein shall ye die; but from it shall ye be taken out (at last)." (7: 19–25).

Mankind is warned of the evil forces and their strong temptations and allurements. This life is a long struggle against all types of contrasts and contradictions. It is a test; the evil one may seduce man. All injustice, iniquity, falsehood, greed, pride, arrogance, oppression and exploitation are represented by the Evil One who 'lies in wait for man'. Only the straight path of truth and righteousness can save man from evil:

"O ye children of Adam let not Satan seduce you in the same manner as he got your parents out of the Garden, stripping them of their raiment to expose their shame: for he and his tribe watch you from a position where ye cannot see them. We made the Evil Ones friends (only) to those who do not believe (in truth). When they do aught that is shameful they say: 'we found our fathers doing so: and God commanded us thus: Say: 'Nay God never commands what is shameful. Do you say of God what ye know not? Say: my Lord hath commanded justice; and that ye set your whole selves (to Him) at every time and place of prayer, and call upon Him, making your devotion sincere as in His sight: such as He created you in the beginning, so shall ye return. Some He hath guided; others have (by their choice) deserved the loss of their way. In that they took the Evil Ones, in preference to God, for their friends and protectors, and think that they receive guidance. (7: 27–30).

Thus the evil forces made the misguided people to follow iniquitous institutions, falsehood, greed, lust and arrogance, whereas God commanded man to be righteous, innocent, truthful and sincere. Those who follow falsehood wrongly think that they are on the right path. They deceive themselves.

Adam is the vice-gerent or deputy, *Wasiy* of God on earth which means that he is endued with talents and powers, faculties and emotions, intellect and conscience. As a perfect vice-gerent he has, like God, will and power to act and initiate, plan and think. The angels or natural powers, according to the metaphors used by the Qur'an, have no will of their own: they only obey certain laws and commands of God.

Adam also excells angels in his knowledge of the inner nature, essences and qualities of things and processes. Knowledge is power and with knowledge man rises to greater heights to control nature and universe. Man has latent powers and faculties. If he suppresses them and does not realize them he falls to the level of animals, and misled and tempted by evil forces he sheds blood and corrupts his qualities and destroys the beautiful world in which he lives:

> "Behold, thy Lord said to the angels: I will create a vice-gerent on earth. They said: wilt Thou place therein one who will make mischief therein and shed blood? Whilst we do celebrate Thy praises and glorify Thy holy (name)"? He said: "I know what ye know not." And He taught Adam the nature of all things, then He placed them before the angels and said: Tell me the nature of these if ye are right. They said: Glory to Thee: of knowledge we have none, save what Thou hast taught us: in truth it is Thou who art perfect in knowledge and wisdom. He said: O Adam! tell them their natures. When he had told them, God said: Did I not tell you that I know the secret of heavens and earth, and I know what ye reveal and what ye conceal. And behold,

We said to the angels: 'Bow down to Adam: and they bowed down: not so Iblis, he refused and was haughty. He was of those who reject (truth)" (2: 30–34).

Man originated from dust as a humble and weak creature but he possesses the faculty of God-like knowledge, will and power the right use of which makes him superior to other creatures. If man remains humble, innocent, honest and truthful, he can rise higher than angels, near to God.

Contrary to man's humble origins, evil originated in arrogance, pride and jealousy. The evil forces subdue only those human beings who succumb to arrogance and jealousy, insolence and selfishness, but they have no power over those who tread the path of truth, innocence, sincerity and honesty, love and selflessness: "Behold; thy Lord said to the angels I am about to create man from sounding clay, from mud moulded into shape. 'When I have fashioned him (in due proportion) and breathed into him of My Spirit, fall ye down in obeisance unto him'. So angels prostrated themselves, all of them together; not so Iblis: he refused to be among those who prostrated themselves." (15: 28–31).

Iblis, Satan or the Evil One represents arrogance and jealousy, the two evils which destroy inner qualities of man. Sincerity to God, according to the Qur'an, means that man can purify himself from all stains of evil and free himself from all temptations and allurements of evil if he follows the path of truth. It changes and transforms inner moral and spiritual faculties and powers of man He has two paths before him: the path of evil and the path of truth. He is free to choose. He is responsible for his actions. If he errs he cannot put blame on Satan, the power of evil. It is the sinner, the falsifier who puts himself into evil's power: "God said: This (way of truth) is indeed a way that leads straight to Me. For over My servants no authority shalt thou (O Satan') have except such as put themselves in the wrong and follow thee." (15: 41–42).

"We had already, before hand, taken the covenant of Adam but he forgot: and We found on his part no firm resolve." (20: 115). . . "Thus did Adam disobey his Lord and allow himself to be seduced." (20: 121) "But his Lord chose him (for His Grace): He turned to him and gave him guidance. He said: 'Get ye down, both of you, all together, from the Garden, with enmity one to another, but if, as is sure, there comes to you guidance from Me, whosoever follows My guidance will not lose his way, nor fall into misery. But whosoever turns away from My Message, verily for him is a life narrowed down and We shall raise him up blind on the Day of Judgement. He will say: 'O my Lord! Why hast Thou raised me up blind, while I had sight (before)? (God) will say: Thus didst thou, when Our Signs came unto thee, disregard them: so wilt thou, this day be disregarded.' And thus do We recompense him who transgresses beyond bounds and believes not in the Signs of his Lord: and the penalty of the Hereafter is far more grievous and more enduring." (20: 122–127).

The first and original man was also a prophet, a wiseman, an intelligent being, an innocent, truthful and humble man of God created from a worthless thing: dust. After his fall he repented and regained his eminence among the creatures and rose to greater heights of intellect, knowledge, will power and reasoning. He gained knowledge and wisdom by which he became able to understand and conquer universe.

Man is the only creature who has emotional and intellectual power, and will of action, inner conscience and initiative to act, explore and understand the inherent laws governing the universe, nature and human society, and qualities and natures, of things and processes.

If man can control his animal instincts and wild passions, i.e. if he shuns evil and walks on the straight path of goodness he can develop his talents, resources and capabilities of his emotion, intellect, conscience and reason. He can in this way rise to a level where he lives in God's presence and where God reveals truth to him as a star of piercing brightness appears in a dark night to show the way.

As he lives under His guidance and light and in His presence, evil forces cannot entice him nor can they have any influence over him. Then he becomes a vice-gerent, a deputy of God's goodness, power, wisdom and knowledge on this earth: "It is He who hath made you (His) agents, inheritors of the earth. He hath raised you in ranks, some above others: that He may try you in the gifts He hath given you; for thy Lord is quick in punishment; yet He is indeed Oft– Forgiving, Most–Merciful"(6:165).

The opposition and struggle between goodness and evil has ever since continued. The next contradiction between these two forces appeared in the lives of Adam's two sons, Habil (Abel) and Qabil (Cain). The former, the younger was righteous, humble, truthful, sincere and innocent. The latter, the elder, was jealous and arrogant, full of rancour and spite against Habil, "Recite to them (O Muhammad!) the

> truth of the story of the two sons of Adam. Behold! they each presented a sacrifice (to God): it was accepted from one but not from the other. Said the latter: Be sure, I will slay thee, 'Surely', said the former, God doth accept of the sacrifice of

those who are righteous, If thou dost stretch thy hand against me to slay me, it is not for me to stretch my hand against thee to slay thee, for I do fear God, the Cherisher of the worlds. For me, I intend to let thee draw on thyself my sin as well as thine, for thou wilt be among the companions of the Fire, and that it is the reward of those who do wrong. The (selfish) soul of the other led him to the murder of his brother: he murdered him, and became (himself) one of the lost ones." (5: 30–33).

8

NUH – THE PROPHET WHO LED THE POOR.

Brute force is a savage and cruel force. It is blind, ferocious, hard-hearted, insensitive and callous. It is without feeling, without remorse, conscience, qualms, pangs or scruples. It is without sympathy and reason, and without pathos, pity or mercy. Whether it is in a beast or in a human being brute force is guided by blind passion, greed, lust and lewdness.

Poverty, or more exactly, relative poverty is an inherent weakness; that is, weakness of resources, lack of economic power, means and media to command other things and rule over men. It is scarcity of economic goods, paucity of political influence and absence of social status, wealth, power and privilges. Wealth is therefore a power and poverty is a weakness. The poor is inherently a weak human being, derided and hated by the rich.

1. Nuh and His Poor Followers:

The poor followers of Nuh (Noah) the great teacher and labourer, were the slaves, orphans, widows, artisans, helpless and weak workers. They appeared to the rich and arrogant brutes of Nuh's community very weak and frail human beings, ragged and wronged, wretched and mean, riff-raffs and worthless scums more fit for carrying burdens like asses and mules, 'hewers of wood and drawers of water.' These poor slaves and workers had revolted against their cruel masters and had gathered round the noble and kind-hearted teacher, the man of God, who taught them truth, human equality, love and brotherhood. The Qur'an says:

> "And We sent Nuh to his people (with a mission): 'I have come to you with a clear warning that ye serve none but God; verily I do fear for you the penalty of a grievous Day. But the chiefs of those who rejected (truth and equality) among his people said: 'We see (in) thee nothing but a man like ourselves. Nor do we see that any follow thee but the meanest among us, in judgement immature. Nor do we see in you (all) any merit above us. In fact we think you are liars." (11: 27).

The powerful rich chiefs who had become impervious to truth, mercy and justice vehemently hated the poor and the slaves. They considered them the pariah, the outcasts and downtrodden who now followed Nuh as a selfless leader and teacher. Nuh organized them into a community of truth and sincerity, love and humility, equality, and brotherhood, compassion and fellow-feeling. The rich approached the leader of the poor to persuade him to disband his 'worthless' gang of weak slaves and artisans. The rich chiefs hated those who earned their living through honest means, with their hands and minds as productive menials. These productive workers were simple, honest, sincere, and kind-hearted.

Their teacher and leader simply replied to the insolent chiefs that they were poor artisans and slaves, helpless and oppressed human beings who came to him to seek sympathy, guidance, truth, love and equality, justice and brotherhood:

"And O my people! I ask you for no wealth in return," so said Nuh to the powerful chiefs, "my reward is from none but God. But I will not drive away (in contempt) those who believe. For verily they are to meet their Lord, and ye I see are the ignorant ones! And O my people! who would help me against God if I drove them away? Will ye not then take heed? I tell you not that with me are the treasures of God, nor do I know what is hidden nor claim I to be an angel. Nor yet do I say of those whom your eyes do despise that God will not give them wealth. God knowest best what is in their souls. I should if I did, indeed be an oppressor (of the poor)". (11: 29–31).

And Nuh refused to compromise with the rich as an oppressor and exploiter of the poor and weak: that is, he boldly rejected their brutal behaviour, their evil and oppressive social order. The chiefs and overlords of Nuh's community had ingeniously devised a false system of religious cults and rites which tended to legitimize the use of brute force by the rich who came to control all wealth, all areas, all means of production, resources, avenues, powers, orders and departments of their society, thus ruthlessly exploiting the poor. They had reduced every poor and weak person to the status of a slave, nay, an animal, a mere beast of burden, a creature of abomination, mean and a wretch. Any one who tried to rise to the level of a free human being among the poor slaves and refused to conform to the official cult was persecuted and killed.

Refusal of Nuh to disband and drive away the army of the poor proletariat and to compromise with their social order of inequality and exploitation, was a challenge to the powerful rulers who saw in their rebel slaves and their leader Nuh a sinister threat to overthrow their power, wealth and privileges. They had erected a beautiful pious facade, nice scaffolding and a superb superstructure of official cults, state religion, beliefs, idols, fancies, imaginations, deceptions, superstitions and lies–a false ideology under whose cover they oppressed and killed, maimed and numbed the poor and the innocent.

They were alarmed and stricken with fear for an imminent revolt would destroy their system. Every brute oppressor is terrified in his inner, hollow heart. The oppressors cried in alarm: save your institutions, customs, religion and temples: "Abandon not your gods, abandon neither Wadd, nor Suwa', neither Yaghuth nor Ya'uq, nor Nasr." "And they devised a tremendous plot" to destroy Nuh and his poor followers (71: 22–23), who were struggling to set up a social order of free and equal human beings, where there were no slaves and masters, no poor and rich, no strong and weak, no oppressed and oppressors; where there was no exploitation, no hatred, no jealousy, arrogance, lust and greed, and no brutal tyrannous force and no selfishness.

2. Worship of Brute Force:

The fetish of nature, astral worship, adoration of powerful animals and human beings and of naked brute force characterized the dominant religious cults of the Mesopotamian society contemporary of Nuh which flourished between the two great rivers, Euphrates and Tigris. The ancient empires of Babylonia and Assyria were based in this extremely fertile region. The famous Flood or Deluge which swept away this society of oppressors and tyrants is historically related to this region.

This adequately shows that among these people the conception of deity or godhead was primitive and was characteristic of the worship of natural forces, their brutality, suddenness and fickleness. These natural forces, rains, rivers, storms and floods deeply influenced the destiny of these people who depended on water and artificial system of irrigation, canals and rivers.

This brought the important element of political, economic and agricultural administration in the ruling religio-political bureaucracy. The ruling cliques and juntas of slave-owners and overlords needed a religio-political ideology of astral and natural worship of brute force to enthral, bewitch and enslave the common people into a fatalistic resignation and passivity. Every ambitious person aspired to become a brute and savage with animal instincts in order to subdue and kill others. This was the chief ideal.

The powerful rich judged others with their own standard and ideal. Those who lacked means of production, wealth, land, slaves and animals and had no political power were considered inferior and despicable human beings. Superior were those who were rich, cruel like a lion, callous like an eagle, sharp and cunning like a horse, and savage like a hard-hearted brute. In this jungle of lawlessness, corruption and brute force, men aspired to become animals. Success was defind as a force to oppress and kill and as skill to exploit the weak, and intellingence meant cunningness, lie and fraud.

The standards of judgement for the arrogant and haughty rulers were thus brute force, selfishness and cunningness. But for Nuh and his followers the standards of judgement were truth, human equality and brotherhood (subsumed under the concept of the Unity of One

God).

Therefore Nuh appeared to the proud slave-owners as a liar, madman, sorcerer, and poet who did not run after lust, power and wealth. In their moral perversity and blindness the powerful rich had become deficient in their faculty of reasoning. Thus in their eyes moral scales were reversed; they erroneously thought that they were on the right path: truth appeared to them as falsehood, equality became inequality, and justice was for them a free license to oppress and kill.

3. The Deluge:

The evil doers had become so insolent and hard-hearted that they refused to listen to Nuh's words of love and wisdom. They spurned in contempt his warning of social chaos, degeneration, war and ultimate destruction of their iniquitous social institutions.

They threatened Nuh that they would stone him to death if he did not desist from his teaching of truth, human equality, justice and brotehrhood. (26: 116). And then a great Flood and Deluge destroyed them utterly. The worshippers and lovers of brute force and tyranny were themselves annihilated by a natural force which encompassed them from all sides, from above and below and they had no way to escape. The Qur'an illustrates this struggle between Nuh and his oppressors in simple parables:

> "It was revealed to Nuh: none of thy people will believe except those who have believed already! So grieve no longer over their (evil) deeds. But construct an Ark under Our eyes and Our inspiration, and address Me no (further) on behalf of those who are in sin; for they are about to be overwhel-

> med (in the Flood). Forthwith he starts constructing the Ark. Every time that the chiefs of his people passed by him threw ridicule on him. He said: If ye ridicule us now, We (in our turn) can look down on you with ridicule likewise"! (11: 36–38).

According to tradition, Nuh lived a long life and preached for truth, justice and equality for over a century to his people. "We sent Nuh to his people and he tarried among them a thousand years less fifty, but the Deluge overwhelmed them while they (persisted in) sin" (29: 15). They perished because they oppressed and killed the poor and weak among them and worshipped brute force and evil as their ideal of a successful life.

> "And the people of Nuh–when they rejected the apostles We drowned them and made them as a sign for mankind; and We have prepared for (all) oppressors (of the poor) grievous penalty"(25: 37).

Nuh's wife and son did not give up relations with the old order. They were also destroyed in the Deluge because in a revolution, in parting of ways with the old corrupt order all old relations of blood, custom, religion, cult, wealth, tribe and family are reversed and severed and only the relations of truth, equality and brotherhood are respected. Nuh's son was not righteous, so he was not a member of the new Brotherhood of Truth and Equality. (11: 15–49.)

The prayer of Nuh just before the Deluge is significant. It shows agony and distress of Nuh wich he felt at the spreading evil ways of the people who did not heed to Nuh's warnings. They considered this wise and noble man a liar and a madman. "O my people", said Nuh to his erring people,

> "I am to you a warner, clear and open: that ye should obev God, fear Him and obey me: so He may

forgive you your sins and give you respite for a stated term. For when the term given by God is accomplished it cannot be put forward if ye only knew." He said: O my Lord! I have called to my people night and day. But my call increases (their) flight (from truth). And every time I have called to them, that Thou mightest forgive them, they have (only) thrust their fingers into their ears, covered themselves up with their garments, grown obstinate, and given themselves up to arrogance. So I have called to them aloud; further I have spoken to them in public and secretly in private–saying, 'ask forgiveness from your Lord, for He is Oft–Forgiving" (71: 2–10).

Oppression, social inequality, schisms and divisions in society destroyed and annihilated the community of the oppressors *Qarya Zalima*. In all its forms, oppression (*Zulm*) cannot endure.

9

HUD – THE PROPHET WHO DEFIED THE ARROGANT'

"To the 'Ad people (We sent), Hud, one of their own brethren. He said: O my people! Obey God! ye have no other god but Him. Will ye not fear (God)? The leaders of those who rejected (truth) among his people said: Ah! we see thou art an imbecile and we think thou art a liar," (7: 65–66).

1. The Class Divisions:

Hud was the prophet-revolutionary who defied the arrogance and brute force of the people of 'Ad who lived in ancient southern Arabia. Their empire extended from 'Uman to Hadramawt and Yemen. They had a great civilization and a prosperous social order. They were tall in stature, strongly built, and were great builders of palaces and temples. Their lands were well-irrigated and they raised rich crops.

But they gradually split up into rich and poor classes. The rich and powerful started oppressing the poor. Their social system decayed, famines and disasters destroyed them.

Hud was a righteous man, a truthful and sincere teacher who invited them to the path of truth and social equality but they refused to follow him. They considered him a stupid person and a liar. "They said: O Hud! no Clear (Sign) hast thou brought us, and we are not the ones to desert our gods on thy word! Nor do we believe in thee. We say nothing but that (perhaps) some of our gods may have siezed thee with imbecility" (11: 53–54).

The arrogant people of 'Ad were proud of their evil ways and corrupt institutions through which they oppressed the weak and the poor. They were also superstitious and thought that, as Hud ridiculed their gods, heroes and religious institutions and ideas, he was being destroyed by them.

They mocked the noble teacher and scoffed at his teachings of truth and social equality. "Such were the 'Ad people who rejected the Signs of their Lord and Cherisher; they disobeyed His Apostles; and followed the command of every powerful, obstinate transgressor." (11: 59).

Hud, the man of God, was defying the proud and insolent people. He told them that their obstinacy and cruelty could not harm truth he was proclaiming. God will destroy them and "will make another people to succeed you, and you will not harm Him in the least." (11: 57). The Qur'an portrays Hud's struggle for truth and equality in some beautiful verses:

> "The 'Ad (people) rejected the apostles. Behold, their brother Hud said to them: 'will ye not fear (God)? I am to you an apostle worthy of all trust. So fear God and obey me. No reward do I ask of you for it: my reward is only from the Lord of worlds. Do ye build a landmark on every high place to amuse yourselves? And do ye get for yourselves fine buildings in the hope of living therein (for ever), And when ye exert your strong hand do ye do it like men of absolute power? Now fear God

and obey me. Yea, fear Him Who has bestowed on you freely all that ye know. Freely has He bestowed on you cattle and sons– and gardens and springs. Truly I fear for you the penalty of a Great Day. They said 'It is the same to us whether thou admonish us or be not among (our) admonishers. This is no other than a customary device of the ancients. And we are not the ones to receive pains and penalties". (26: 123–138).

2. Arrogance of the Rich:

Arrogance or pride in the rich and powerful is a sort of falsehood which unduly assumes and claims things, powers and privileges without any right but with brute force. It is a passion of greed and lust which is based on selfishness. A selfish brute is a blind person, rather a lustful beast who destroys others for selfish ends. The acquisitive lust does not fill the appetite, and the animal desire has no end.

Arrogance is the enemy of truth, humility, patience, love and sincerity. The gods which the arrogant people of 'Ad worshipped were lust, greed and selfishness. This had made them hard–hearted and insolent. When every one runs after his own selfish ends the society begins to rot because pride and selfishness kill natural talents and capabilities of human beings by turning them into beasts and brutes who persecute and kill their own fellows. This is suicidal and detrimental for a community of human beings. The weak and the poor, the slaves, the women, workers, orphans and old people have no place in such a social order: "Mention (Hud) one of 'Ad's own brethren. Behold, he warned his people around the winding sand-tracts: but there have been warners before him and after him: 'obey ye none other than God; truly I fear for you the penalty of a Mighty Day'. They said: 'Hast thou come in order to turn us aside from our gods? Then bring upon us the (calamity) with which thou dost threaten us, if thou art telling the truth'! He said: 'The knowledge (of when it will come), is only with God: I proclaim to you the Mission on which I have been sent. But I see that ye are a people (steeped) in ignorance'! Then, when they saw the (penalty in the shape of) a cloud traversing the sky, coming to meet their valleys, they said, 'This cloud will give us rain!' 'Nay, it is the (Calamity) ye were asking to be hastened,–a wind wherein is a grievous penalty! Everything will it destroy by the command of its Lord! Then by the morning they–nothing was to be seen but (the ruins of) their houses. Thus do We recompense those given to sin. And We had firmly established them in a (prosperity and) power which We have not given to you (ye Quresh of Mecca!) and We had endowed them with (faculties of) hearing, seeing, heart and intellect. But of no profit to them were their (faculties of) hearing, sight and heart and intellect, when they went on rejecting the Signs of God; and they were (completely) encircled by that which they used to mock at!" (46: 21–26; see also 54: 18–22; 89: 6–9).

The 'Ad were a talented people. They had fine intellects, robust physiques and health. They had built up a refined civilization and a prosperously rich social order. But they misused their natural qualities and wasted their talents in false pursuits, in selfish ways, lusts and animal passions. They oppressed the poor and killed the weak. This was self-annihilation, because when people start killing each other they weaken the moral and social structures. The prople of 'Ad were like a person who takes his own passion for his god. They worshipped their own passions, impulses and desires of selfishness and greed.

This animal passion destroys intellect and rational, moral and emotional powers in man. A selfish and arrogant man is worse than a beast. This leads to callousness and lawlessness. A brute has no feelings and no pangs of conscience. He has no criterion to judge right from wrong and good from evil.

In a society where brute force rules and where distinictions of right and wrong, good and bad are blotted out and differences blurred, only those people can survive in the jungle who are powerful. All run to acquire power. This power may be of several types. It may be a physical power which can resist attacks of others and can do whatever it likes. Economic power or power of wealth and money can also give strength to the person who acquires it.

Money or wealth is actually a command over things and persons: the rich person can buy things and slaves and cattle; he can buy influence, political and social privileges, status, prestige and power. One can have manpower, mercenaries, force of sons, brothers and his tribal people. This craze for power drives men to acquire all these forms of strength. Possession of power, wealth, men and things makes rich people greedy and arrogant.

The prophet-revelutionary is divinely inspired. He is a criterion for making distinctions between right and wrong, good and bad. He seeks strength from the divine source, from truth and humility, from sincerity and selflessness, and from social equality, and justice.

Hud defied power and arrogance of the 'Ad with his

power of truth and social equality, with the power of his dedicated followers, the power of high moral principles. As these poor people avoided all greed and acquisitive passions to accumulate wealth, they were considered by their rich enemies as madmen and liars. Their revolutionary leader was termed a sorcerer, insane and abnormal person. But Hud humbly replied "O my people! I am not a stupid person or an imbecile, but (I am) an apostle from the Lord and Cherisher of the worlds! I but fulfil towards you the duties of my Lord's mission: I am to you a sincere and trustworthy adviser. Do you wonder that there hath come to you a message from your Lord through a man of your own people to warn you? Call in remembrance that He made you inheritors after the people of Nuh, and gave you a stature tall among the nations. Call in remembrance the benefits (ye have received) from God: that so ye may prosper" (7: 67–69).

But the arrogant people did not heed the warning of Hud; their mutual hatred, selfishness, lust and pride drove them towards social and moral chaos and destruction. "But those who reject Our Signs and treat them with arrogance, they are companions of the Fire to dwell therein (for ever)". (7: 36).

10

SȦLIH AND HIS FIGHT FOR SOCIAL EQUALITY.

Salih was a righteous and a noble man. He was a great leader and a prophet-revolutionary who fought against nine powerful familes, tribes or groups of rich and arrogant people who forcibly got hold of common lands, pastures and springs and drove out the weak and poor to starvation and death. Salih led the poor against the forces of inequality and injustice. The Qur'an recounts Salih's fight against the powerful oppressors in the following words:

> "We sent (aforetime) to the Thamud, their brother Salih saying, 'serve God': but behold, they became two factions quarrelling with each other. He said: 'O my people! why ask ye to hasten on the evil in preference to the good! If only ye ask God for forgiveness, ye may hope to receive mercy'. They said: 'Ill omen do we augur from thee'! He said: 'your ill omen is with God; yea, ye are a people under trial'. There were in the city nine men or groups of people who spread corruption in the land and would not reform. They said: 'swear a mutual oath by God that we shall make a secret night attack on him and his people and that we shall then say to his heir (when he seeks vengeance): 'We were not present at the slaughter of his people and we are positively telling the truth.' They plotted and

> planned but We too planned, even while they perceived not. Then see what was the end of their plot!—this, that We destroyed them and their people, all (of them). Now such were their houses, —in utter ruin—because they oppressed (the poor): verily in this is a Sign for people of knowledge. And We saved those who believed (in truth) and practised righteousness." (27: 45–53).

1. The Nine Rich Families:

The nine groups of oppressors tried to kill the poor people and their prophet-revolutionary, Salih, because they dared to challenge their oppressive social order. They planned and conspired but such intrigues and false plans do not succeed against the righteous.

The people of Thamud inherited the culture and civilization, prosperity and wealth of the people of 'Ad. Their ancestor was probably called Thamud, the son of Abir, a brother of Aram, son of Sam, son of Noah (Nuh). The lands of the people of Thamud lay in the north—western part of Arabia, anciently known as Arabia Petraea. The land was fertile and consisted of fields, common pastures, and springs.

With the growth of wealth and prosperity the pastoral-tribal social order split up into two broad social classes: the powerful rich and the poor proletariat. The former came to monopolize all means of production, land and water resources and thus began oppressing those who were dispossessed. Salih, the courageous teacher challenged this monopoly of the powerful families. He exposed the weaknesses, internal contradictions, contrasts and evils of the regime of social inequality.

Common lands, pastures and water were common property belonging to all, so asserted Salih. To carve private property was selfishness, a sin and a crime against the whole community. What was for the use of all the creatures of God could not be possessed by a few powerful men with brute force. He declared the plain truth:

> "O my people!" he urged, "Obey God; ye have no other god but Him. Now hath come unto you a clear (Sign) from your Lord! This she-camel of God is a Sign unto you, so leave her to graze in God's earth (i.e. common land), and let her come to no harm. Or ye shall be seized with a grievous punishment" (7: 73).

Salih was a wise and bold man. He led a simple and honest life. He lieved with the simple, ordinary and poor people of Thamud. He taught them truth, honesty and love of mankind. He was a champion of social equality. The powerful rich who ruled over the land tried hard to win him over to their corrupt ways of life, to falsehood, evil, greed and arrogance.

They were ready to make him their leader, a rich man, a king or a governor with power and anthority provided he compromised with the institutions, religious and social ideology of their oppressive social order of acute socio-economic inequality. "They said: O Salih! thou hast been of us! a centre of our hopes hitherto! Dost thou (now) forbid us the worship of what our fathers worshipped? But we are really in suspicious (disquieting) doubt as to that to which thou invitest us". (11: 62). But Salih was a fighter for truth and a champion of the cause of the poor who had been driven out of the common lands. He was an enemy of selfish privileges and monopolization of common lands, pastures, and water resources.

He led the dispossessed and challenged the powerful

oppressors to allow the flocks and herds of the weak tribes to graze on the common lands otherwise they would destroy their iniquitous social order and their exclusive monopoly of land and water which were free gifts of nature. "And O my people"! said Salih, "this she–camel is a symbol to you. Leave her to feed on God's (free) earth, and inflict no harm on her, or a swift penalty will seize you! But they did hamstring her. So he said: 'Enjoy yourselves in your homes for three days (then will be your ruin). There is a promise not to be belied! When Our Decree issued We saved Salih and those who believed in (truth and equality) with him, by (special) Grace from Ourselves–and from the ignominy of that Day. For the Lord–He is the Strong One, and Able to enforce His Will. The (mighty) Blast overtook the oppressors, and they lay prostrate in their homes before the morning." (11: 64–67).

2. The Social Order of Inequality:

The social order of inequality is a frail structure. The nine powerful groups or tribes who had occupied common lands and means of production drove out the weak tribes and groups. They starved and weakened the majority of the people. When the whole community becomes weak and feeble it is an open invitation to the more powerful marauders living around this weak community. The ruling nine groups also weakened themselves because of corruption, greed, lust and selfishness, pride and arrogance. Evil made them effete.

This general weakness of all the social classes corroded the inner moral vitality of the entire community. Salih pointed out the weaknesses and contrasts of their unequal social order. He was alarmed to see the glaring contradictions of brute force and powerlessness, riches and poverty, indulgence of the rich nine families and misery and hunger of the weak tribes. The injustice, exploitation and hard-heartedness of the powerful filled him with anger and dismay. He said to them by way of admonition:

> "Will ye be left secure in (the enjoyment of) all that ye have? – gardens and springs and corn-fields and date-palms with spathes near breaking (with the weight of fruit)? And ye carve houses out of (rocky) mountains with great skill. Then fear God and obey me; and follow not the bidding of those who exceed all bounds, who spread corruption in the land and mend not (their ways)". They said: 'Thou art only one of those bewitched. Thou art no more than a mortal like us. Then bring us a Sign if thou tellest the truth'. He said: 'Here is a she-camel; she has a right of watering, and ye have a right of watering, (severally) on a day appointed (in the common spring)." (26: 146–155).

Salih's challenge was a threat to the corrupt social order which was presided over by the nine families and their lords, chiefs and priests. The poor stood up under the prophet-revolutionary to assert for their rights over the common lands, pastures and water which were in the possession of the powerful rulers. The corrupt chiefs and lords after failing in their efforts to bribe the rebel, now started accusing him of being a madman, a mischief-monger and a rabble-rouser.

Whenever prophets and revolutionaries waged war against evil and oppression they were labelled as sorcerers, soothsayers, poets, madmen and foreign agents because the oppressors cannot justify their corrupt social order on any moral or human grounds. Therefore they decide to destroy those who callenge to destabilize their weak social order. So the nine powerful families decided to kill Salih and his movement of social equality and justice. They rejected Salih and his poor followers. "The Thamud rejected their warners. For they said: What! a man! a solitary one from among ourselves! Shall we follow such a one? Truly should we then be straying in mind, and mad. Is it that the Message is sent to *him;* of all people amongst us; Nay, he is a liar, an insolent one." (54: 23–26).

The erring people of Thamud had lost all nobler values. They had fallen in superstition, .perversity, self-complacency and pride. They laughed at Salih and ridiculed his honesty, truthfulness and humility. They thought that his simplicity and humility were weaknesses and his wisdom insanity. They were averse to truth, honesty and sincerity. Therefore they could not understand and appreciate the truth and wisdom brought to them by the prophet-revolutionary.

But Salih had to be patient, persevering and steadfast in his fight against the well-entrenched oppressors who had strengthened themselves through various social, economic, religious and ideological institutions. He calmly preached the message of truth and equality, love and brotherhood. He had inner peace and contentment and he never wavered on his path of righteousness. He was ridiculed in several ways. People mocked derisively at his poverty, simplicity and tenacity of will and purpose. He went on organizing the poor in a community of dedicated believers in the cause of truth. And at last he threw to the insolent rulers the ultimatum: that rights over the use of common lands and waters be given back to the suffering people: "And tell them that the water is to be divided between them; each one's right to drink being brought forward (by suitable turns). But they called to their companion, and he took a sword in hand, and hamstrung (the she-camel). Ah! how terrible was My Penalty and My warning. For We sent against them a single Mighty Blast, and they became like the dry stubble used by one who pens cattle." (54: 28–31).

In the Sura al-Shams (The Sun: 91) the Qur'an says that every human being in this world is born with an inner pure soul, natural clean conscience or the inner moral faculty which is divine and which can distinguish between good and bad, and right and wrong, piety and impiety, equality and inequality, love and oppression.

This is the most precious divine faculty, insight or gift given to human beings. If they keep this inner faculty pure and unstained they can rise to greater heights and can attain prosperity, success and salvation. But those who corrupt this faculty through impiety, oppression and other evil ways, they decay and perish as was the case with the cruel people of Thamud who rejected the divine message of truth and equality, brought to them by their teacher Salih. "The Thamud (people) rejected (their prophet-revolutionary) through their inordinate wrong-doing", says the Qur'an, "behold, the most wicked man among them was deputed (for impiety). But the apostle of God said to them: 'It is a she-camel of God! And (bar her not from) having her drink!' Then they rejected him (as a false prophet), and they hamstrung her. So their Lord, on account of their crime, obliterated their traces and made them equal (in destruction, high and low). And for him (Salih) is no fear of its consequences." (91: 11–15).

Salih as a divinely inspired and guided revolutionary had no fears about the consequences of Thamud's social destruction. He had warned the oppressors of the results and bad effects of their immoral social inequality. He was saved for he was s just and honest person.

As long as the people of Thamud were alive they continued perpetuating their system of inequality and tyranny. They split up into antagonistic social classes and groups. The powerful oppressed the weak and forcibly took hold of the common means of production and sustenanc. They drove out the poor from the common pastures, gardens and springs of water and reduced them to a state of penury, utter ruin, starvation and death.

So death, destruction, revolution and obliteration made them equal at last. They were made dust and their institutions, ideas, passions, lusts, desires, pride and arrogance were all reduced to dust. According to the Qur'an, social orders based on corruption, injustice, inequality and false ideas are inherently weak and are likely to be destroyed by internal contradictions, schisms, dissensions or by the more powerful and equalitarian social orders.

11

IBRAHIM – THE PROPHET WHO PROCLAIMED TRUTH AND JUSTICE

"O people of the Book!", says the Qur'an to the Jews and Christians contemporary of prophet Muhammad, "Why dispute ye about Ibrahim when the Torah (The Law) and the Evangel (the Gospel) were not revealed till after him? Have ye no understanding? Ah! ye are those who fell to disputing (even) in matters of which ye had some knowledge; But why dispute ye in matters of which ye have no knowledge? It is God who knows and ye who know not! Ibrahim was not a Jew, nor yet a Christian; but was a man of truth and submitted his will to God's Will and he joined not gods with God" (3: 65–67).

1. The True Man of God:

Ibrahim was a true man of God, a prophet-revolutionary who revolted against a god-king. He struggled all his life for truth and justice. He suffered at the hands of his oppressors. He left his home for the sake of his cause and migrated to another country where he succeeded in establishing a community of truth and justice, love and equality.

He was neither a Jew, nor a Christian but a righteous man, a courageous leader and a bold fighter for justice.

He was a man of noble character, and he rightly became a model for prophet Muhammad and his revolutionaries in Arabia:

> "Ibrahim was indeed a model, devoutly obedient to God, and true in faith and he joined not gods with Him. He showed his gratitude for the favours of God, who chose him, and guided him to a straight path. And We gave him Good in this world, and he will be, in the Hereafter, in the ranks of the Righteous. So We have taught thee (O Muhammad) the inspired (message): 'Follow the ways of Ibrahim, the true in faith and he joined not gods with God." (16: 120–123).

For centuries, the noble personality of Ibrahim, the great prophet-revolutionary, his teachings, struggles and sacrifices for the cause of truth, justice and salvation of suffering humanity and emancipation of the weak from falsehood and oppression, have occupied a prominent place in the social and religious history of mankind.

Ibrahim was a great prophet, a divinely-inspired, courageous fighter against the forces of evil, darkness and superstition. He was a bold man, a kind-hearted friend, lover of the weak, a noble patriarch, an honest and truthful, bold warrior against tyrants, oppressors and exploiters of the poor. He never compromised on principles and always stood alone like a rock against the forces of evil.

According to the Qur'an Ibrahim was a man of truth who followed the true path (*hanif*) of justice and social equality, love and brotherhood. He followed *Islam* (literally surrender of a truthful man to the will of God. i.e. truth, equality and justice) as all prophets were *muslims* in so far as they stood for truth and fought against oppressors of the weak. "There is for you," says the Qur'an to the revolutionaries who followed prophet Muhammad, "an excellent example (to follow) in Ibrahim and those with him, when they said to their people: 'We are clear of you and of whatever ye obey besides God; we have rejected you, and there has arisen, between us and you enmity and hatred for ever,—— unless ye believe in God and Him alone'.– (60: 4).

And God stood with Ibrahim and all natural, moral and historical forces stood with him and his followers because they were on the right path. But who was prophet Ibrahim? What was his cause or social mission? Who were his enemies? Why did he migrate to Palestine and leave his hearth and home behind? why did he become a model for prophet Muhammad and for the early Muslim revolutionaries?

The Qur'an portrays him as "without doubt, forbearing (of faults), compassionate and given to look to God." (11:75). He was 'most tender-hearted, forbearing.' (9: 114). He had three chief traits of his character: he was kind-hearted and long-suffering with other people's faults and failings, (2) his sympathies, loves, and compassion were for all, (3) and in sorrow, pain, suffering and adversity he turned to God and sought Him in humility, gratitude and prayer. His way was the way of truth. "And who turns away from the way of life of Ibrahim but such as debase their souls with folly? Him We chose and rendered pure in this world: and he will be in the Hereafter in the ranks of the righteous. Behold! his Lord said to him: 'Bow (thy will to Me'); He said: 'I bow (my will) to the Lord and Cherisher of the Universe". (2: 130–131).

Great civilizations flourished and decayed in the fertile plane between the two great rivers, Euphrates and Tigris. Almost thirteen centureis before the birth of Jesus

Christ, there ruled in the land of the Chaldees certain Semitic tribes who had changed from nomads and settled as agriculturists, built cities, fortresses and temples. The country of Chaldea stretched from the Gulf to the borders of Arabian desert. This empire later declined and fell into a morass of moral turpitude, corruption, religious and social tyranny. The whole populace was astray and worshipped heavenly hierarchies, Sun, moon, stars and fire. There were so many gods–human, natural objects and idols, on whose head stood the god-king whose word was law and whose decree was final, and who considered himself all-powerful.

Brute force was thus the law of the land and the poor and weak people were treated as slaves and drudges. An acute sense of fear and insecurity, superstitious cults and rituals had all made people to bow down before rich and powerful chiefs and lords. This had destroyed the moral and social fabric and had unleashed a reign of terror.

According to the Biblical tradition*, Abram (later changed into Abraham or Ibrahim), Nahur and Haran were three sons of Terah (Azar). Azar was probably the official high priest who made and sold idols, thus tying his economic power and privileges with the official religious ideology. Their home was in the city of Ur (which means a flame in Hebrew) in Chaldea. When after some time Abram became a prophet, revolted against the oppressors and united the warring tribes into a single united community he began to be called Ibrahim (Abraham). In Aramaic, *abir* meant chief and *ham* was a multitude or crowd, that is, a chief or patriarch of people.

The details of Ibrahim's birth and childhood are not

* According to the Bible, Ibrahim was the son of Tarih b. Nahur b. Sarugh b. Reu b. Faligh b. Abir b. Shalikh b. Qainan b. Arfakhshad b. Sam b. Nuh.

known but a legend says that when he was born, the god-king Namrud ordered his father to handover the babe to the king in order to be killed. He was saved and in his place the son of a slave woman was killed. He was probably brought up in a cave or a village remote from the city of the god-king. Ibrahim's childhood and youth remained safe from the corrupting influences of the immoral and sinful ways of the Chaldeans. He hated the corrupt ways of the people, their oppressive institutions and superstitious religion and cults. "Lo! Ibrahim said to his father Azar: "Takest thou idols for gods? For I see thee and thy people in manifest error. So also did We show Ibrahim the power and the laws of the heavens and the earth, that he might (with understanding) have certitude." (6: 74–75).

2. Ibrahim Discovers the Truth:

Ibrahim grew up among the Chaldeans who had great knowledge of astronomy and astrology because they worshipped stars and heavenly bodies. From ancient times Chaldeans were known as 'wise men' for their knowledge of heavenly bodies and their movements. After his call to prophethood and after his divine inspiration be meditated on the real factors and causes of the moral and socio-economic degeneration of his community. He explored what lay beyond the physical-social phenomenon. He rejected the official religious cults and rituals; and this meant a revolt against the god-king and the corrupt socio-economic institutions, ideas and practices. Ibrahim discovered the laws and principles governing the universe. He found out the reasons of his community's social decay and moral death.

For him the root-cause of the corruption, tyranny

and oppression of the weak human beings, groups and classes was the fear of the god-king and the powerful oppressors which bred falsehood and evil in the people' minds and hearts. To bow before human beings, before idols of heros, idols of lusts and passions, desires and greeds, falsehood and dark impulses, self-love and pride was sure way to destruction and annihilation because such a slavish and perversive behaviour was divesting his community of courage, truth, honesty, equality and love. Ibrahim discovered this truth as a scholar-prophet. This dawned on his mind gradually. He discovered truth in suffering and persecution, in a gradual process. He had seen that corruption, evil and oppression had darkened and hardened the minds and hearts of his people. They could not distinguish right from wrong and true from false. His discovery of ultimate truth is described by the Qur'an in its beautiful allegorical style:

> "When the night covered him over, he saw a star. He said: 'This is my Lord'. But when it set, he said: 'I love not those who set. When he saw the moon rising in splendour, he said: 'This is my Lord'. But when the moon set, he said: 'unless my Lord guide me, I shall surely be among those who go astray. When he saw the sun rising in splendour, he said: 'This is my Lord; this is the greatest (of all)'. But when the sun set, he said: 'O my people: I am now free from your (sin of) associating (human beings and idols) with (powers and attributes of) God. For me, I have set my face (my whole self), firmly and truly, towards Him who created the heavens and the earth, and never shall I give partners to God. His people disputed with him. He said (come) ye to dispute with me, about God, when He (Himself) hath guided me, I fear not (the beings) ye

> associate with God. Unless my Lord willeth (nothing can happen). My Lord comprehendeth in His knowledge all things. Will ye not (yourselves) be admonished"? (6: 76–80).

Ibrahim declared the truth he had discovered in plain terms. He pronounced boldly that he rejected the god-king, the chiefs and lords,—the oppressors of the poor masses; and that he revolted against their immoral ways of life, their corrupt social system, their unjust institutions and their superstitious religion which had falsely attributed powers to the corrupt human beings, and thus had misguided the people.

3. War against Injustice:

This was actually a declaration of war against the forces of evil and corruption, against inequality, and injustice, against the economic and political power of the rulers and their false laws. He was tempted but he never wavered on the path of truth. He persevered and remained patient in persecutions. All left him. The corrupt rulers humiliated him. Even his father and his family and tribe abandoned him to be persecuted and killed. Only his wife, Sarah, and nephew Lut (Lot) stood with him in the hour of danger. Because he dissented with the oppressors, they threatened him with death. But he would not care.

He had found out the truth and was strongly convinced that he was on the right path. He was free from superstitions, false desires, false hopes and false possessions. Now that he was opposing oppression he invited them to embrace his truth, be honest and courageous obeying the one supreme God (i.e. truth and social equality). He challenged them that as he followed truth he was rightly guided and that oppression and iniquity had no grounds:

> "How should I fear (the beings) ye associate with God, when ye fear not to give partners to God without any authority having been given to you? Which of us two parties hath more right to security? (tell me) if ye know. It is those who believe (in truth) and confuse not their beliefs with wrong–that are (truly) in security, for they are on right guidance". (6: 81–82).

The god-king was intoxicated with power. He had political authority over people and lands. He considered himself al-mightly and that none was superior to him. This was sheer arrogance. On the other hand, Ibrahim was a man of God: he had faith in a power which sustains all and nourishes all and who is the fountain-head of all power. "Hast thou (O Muhammad!) not turned thy vision to one who disputed with Ibrahim about his Lord, because God had granted him Power (of dominion)? Ibrahim said: My Lord is He who giveth life and death. He said: 'I give life and death'. Ibrahim said: 'But it is God that causeth the sun to rise from the East: do thou then cause it to rise from the west'. Thus was he confounded who (in arrogance) rejected (truth and equality). Nor doth God give guidance to a people unjust." (2: 258).

Ibrahim was a dedicated prophet-revolutionary. He was devoted to truth and justice. The people of Chaldea tenaciously clung to the depraved social and economic institutions and blindly followed the rotten customs and immoral traditions of their ancestors. When war broke out between him and the oppressors he was threatened of dire cousequences for his attacking of their false religion and gods. But he was undaunted and fearless. He feared only God and nothing else. He was wise, courageous and humble:

> "We bestowed aforetime on Ibrahim his rectitude of conduct, and well were We acquainted with him. Behold! he said to his father and his people, 'What are these images to which ye are (so assiduously) devoted? They said: 'we found our fathers worshipping them? He said: 'indeed, ye have been in manifest error–ye and your fathers. They said, 'Have you brought us the Truth or are you one of those who jest?' He said, 'Nay, your Lord is the Lord of the heavens and the earth. He who created them (from nothing); and I am a witness to this (truth). And by God, I have a plan for your idols–after ye go away and turn your backs'. . So he broke them to pieces (all) but the biggest of them, that they might turn (and address themselves) to it. They said, 'Who has done this to our gods? He must indeed be some man of impiety! They said, 'we heard a youth talk of them: he is called Ibrahim. They said: 'Then bring him before the eyes of the people, that they may bear witness. They said: Art thou the one that did this with our gods O Ibrahim?' He said: 'Nay, this was done by this their biggest one! Ask them, if they can speak intelligently." (21: 51–63).

Ibrahim was presented before the High Tribunal and was tried and sentenced to death. He was declared guilty of trying to destroy the established social order and of harming the official religion, their gods and social stability and peace. He was a rebel who was inciting the oppressed to overthrow the corrupt social order. "They said: 'Burn him and protect your gods if ye do (anything at all)"! (21: 68). And he was thrown into the fire. "We said, O Fire! Be thou cool and (a means of) safety for Ibrahim"! "Then they sought a stratagem against him, but We made them the ones that lost most." (21: 69–70).

He was now declared a rebel and was persecuted, and thrown into a burning furnace but he was saved. They could not kill him. Then they thought upon various stratagems to remove him from their midst. It appears that his humiliations and persecutions increased and his enemies started spending all their energies to get rid of him. He decided to migrate to the west, to the fertile land of Aram or Syria and then to the south to the land of Canaan in Palestine. At that time Palestine was a province of Egypt.

His struggle against the oppressors and his decision to migrate are beautifully described in other verses of the Qur'an:

"(Also) mention in the Book (the story of) Ibrahim. He was a man of truth, a prophet. Behold, he said to his father: O my father why worship that which heareth not and seeth not, and can profit thee nothing? O my father! to me hath come knowledge which hath not reached thee. So follow me, I will guide thee to a way that is even and straight. O my father, serve not Satan: for Satan is a rebel against (God) Most Gracious. O my father! I fear lest a penalty afflict thee from (God) Most Gractious, so that thou become to Satan a friend. (The father) replied: 'Dost thou hate my gods, O Ibrahim? If thou forbear not, I will indeed stone thee (to death). Now get away from me for a good long while? Ibrahim said: 'peace be on thee: I will pray to my Lord for thy frogiveness; for He is to me Most Gracious. And I will turn away from you (all) and from those whom ye invoke besides God. I will call on my Lord; perhaps, by my prayer to my Lord I shall not be unblest. When he had turned away from them and from those whom they worshipped besides God, We bestowed on him Ishaq (Isaac) and Ya'qub (Jacob) and each one of them We made a prophet. And We bestowed of our Mercy on them, and We granted them lofty honour on the tongue of truth." (19: 41–50).

4. The Great Migration:

So Ibrahim left his father, his tribe and home in Ur, in Chaldea for good for the cause of truth for which he was struggling. He did not compromise with the rulers, with the god-king and his father. This cause of truth is the most precious thing in the world. To fight for truth, human equality, love and brotherhood is to struggle for the 'way of God,' and in the words of the Qur'an, "If ye are slain, or die in the way of God, forgiveness and mercy from God are far better than all they (rejecters of truth) could amass." (3: 157).

This was the Great Migration, *Hijra,* of Ibrahim, for upholding the cause of truth. This Hijra is the common feature of the struggles of the prophet-revolutionaries who fought against falsehood and corruption and never compromised. (19: 30–40, 41–50, 51–53, 54–55, 56–65).

His wife Sarah and nephew Lut accompanied him in his hour of trial. They believed in his truth and remained with him in his travails and tribulations. In Palestine, he lived in the coastal region of Canaan with his flocks of sheep and goats, wandering from pasture to pasture and fighting against tyrants and god-kings of various places.

Ibrahim became a great prophet-revolutionary, a patriarch, a kind-hearted fighter of truth and justice, a man of truth (*Hanif*), friend of God (*Khalil Allah*) who bowed to none but God and feared none but God. He was now childless and Sarah urged him to wed her Egyptian slave-girl Hajira (Hagar) as he worried about his heirs.

Ten years after his entry into Canaan when he was about eighty six years old a son was born to Hajira and was named Isma'il. When Ibrahim was hundred years old another son, Ishaq, was born to Sarah. According to the Biblical tradition, Sarah was harsh to Hajira and her son.

After a long famine Ibrahim wandered in search of green pastures and went towards Egypt where he had to face acute problems and difficulties at the hands of the Egyptian king and lords. But he ultimately triumphed over them with his resolute faith, patience and perseverance.

At last, Ibrahim and his nephew Lut, who also rose to be a prophet-revolutionary, returned from Egypt to the district of Bethel. Their flocks and herds increased and they became powerful. With the increase in population, wealth and flocks this community broke up into two large groups, one following the patriarch and the other gathered around Lut. The two chiefs agreed to separate and part ways.

Lut left for the rich pastures of the Jordan valley and Ibrahim settled on a less fertile land. Lut was later rejected by the corrupt people of Sodom and Gomorrah. This land of the depraved was attacked by the king of Elam and his vassal kings and Lut was carried away as a prisoner of war. Ibrahim reorganized his army and defeated the enemy in the north of Canaan and freed Lut. Ibrahim then established himself in the south of Canaan, in Hebron and Beersheba and formed confederates with local tribes. Here he united various tribes under the banner of truth, equality and brotherhood.

According to the Qur'an the Patriarch took Hajira and Isma'il to Arabia and came to the barren valley of Mecca. Mecca contained the sanctuary of Ka'ba. "The first Houe (of worship) appointed for men was that of Bakka, full of blessing and of guidance for all kinds of beings" (3: 96). "Behold! We gave the site to Ibrahim, of the (Sacred House) (saying): 'Associate not anything (in worship) with Me; and sanctify My House for those who compass it round, or stand up or bow, or prostrate themselves (therein in prayer). And proclaim the pilgrimage among men; they will come to thee on foot and (mounted) on every kind of camel, lean on account of journeys through deep and distant mountain highways, that they may witness the benefits (provided) for them, and celebrate the name of God, through the days, appointed, over the cattle which He has provided for them (for sacrifice): then eat ye thereof and feed the distressed ones in want (and hunger)". . : . (22: 26–28).

When Ibrahim came to Mecca he found it a barren-land where there was no cultivation. The hearts, minds and souls of the people were also barren and despoiled by all sorts of evils, internecine wars, falsehoods and superstitions. He united the tribes around his proclaimed truth of one God, human equality and brotherhood. He reformed the people, established an equalitarian social order. "Remember Ibrahim said:"

> "O my Lord! make this city one of peace and security, and preserve me and my sons from worshipping idols. O my Lord! they have indeed led astray many among mankind. He then who follows my (way of life) is of me and he that disobeys me,– but thou art indeed Oftforgiving, Most Merciful. O our Lord! I have made some of my offspring to dwell in a

valley without cultivation, by Thy Sacred House. In order, O our Lord, that they may establish prayer, so fill the hearts of some among men with love towards them, and feed them with fruits so that they may give thanks." (14: 35–37).

Throughout his life and his struggles for the cause of truth, Ibrahim remained steadfast. He never slackened his efforts, nor did he lose heart in difficulties and trials. He was long-suffering and forbearing for the faults of other human being. He was a great prophet-revolutionary and was rightly made a model by prophet Muhammad. (16: 120–123).

"And remember that Ibrahim was tried by his Lord with certain commands which he fulfilled. He said: I will make thee a leader of the people. He pleaded: And also (leaders) from my offspring!' He answered: 'But my Promise is not within the reach of oppressors. Remember We made the House a place of assembly for men and a place of safety. And take ye the station of Ibrahim as a place of prayer; and We covenanted with Ibrahim and Ismail, that they should sanctify My House for those who compass it round, or use it as a retreat, or bow or prostrate themselves (therein in prayer). And remember Ibrahim said: 'My Lord, make this a city of peace, and feed its people, with fruits–such of them as believe in God and the Last Day'. He said: '(yea), and such as reject (truth) – for a while will I grant them their pleasure, but will soon drive them to the torment of Fire–an evil destination (indeed)'! (2: 124–126).

The truth which Ibrahim discovered and then taught throughout his life was that real power belongs to God; He is the source of all knowledge, wisdom, sustenance, power, goodness and mercy; to Him belongs every thing in the Universe. Human beings must submit to the Will and Plan of God as every thing submits to Him according to its inherent laws. One who submits to idols, powerful heros, human beings, kings and lords or to one's own whims, desires, passions, greed and lusts, deviates from the path of truth. One who does not fear God fears every thing:

> "And (We also saved) Ibrahim: behold, he said to his people, 'Serve God and fear Him; that will be best for you–if ye understand, for ye do worship idols besides God and ye invent falsehood. The things that ye worship besides God have no power to give you sustenance: Then seek ye sustenance from God, serve Him: and be grateful to Him; to Him will be your return. And if ye reject (the Message of this truth), so did generations before you; and the duty of the apostle is only to preach publicly (and clearly)". (29: 16–18).

This great prophet-revolutionary and man of truth and justice became an excellent example for later prophets, saints and men of God who strove to establish just and equalitarian communities. His fortitude, his trust in his Creator and firm belief in the unity and equality of mankind made his noble personality a model for generations. The early Muslim revolutionaries were proud to be the followers of Ibrahim, the Patriarch.

He was the shining model, and the beacon light for them and a character to be emulated in adversity and prosperity, in revolution and in peace – "There is for you an excellent example (to follow) in Ibrahim and those with him," says the Qur'an to the revolutionaries of prophet Muhammad, "when they said to their people: 'we are clear of you and of whatever ye worship besides

God: we have rejected you, and there has arisen between us and you, enmity and hatred for ever,—unless ye believe in God and Him alone," (60: 4).

A tradition says that Ibrahim refused to obey the commands of king Namrud to the effect that he should worship fire and conform to the official religion and the established institutions and customs. This happened in Chaldea which Ibrahim left for ever. It is also said that he had conquered Damascus and that he popularized the knowledge of arithmetic which he had learnt in Chaldea, and astrology in Egypt. He was a great scholar, a prophet-revolutionary, a leader, a judge and a patriarch who changed the social and cultural history of the Near East. He is reported to have died at the age of 175 and was buried in the cave of Machpelah.

His son Isma'il was also a great prophet-revolutionary, a man of God, "he was (strictly) true to what he promised," says the Qur'an, "and he was an apostle and a prophet." (19: 54). Ibrahim loved God more than any thing else and he did every thing to please Him: this is true Islam. Isma'il was an obedient and patient son. Their lofty characters have been explained allegorically by the Qur'an. Ibrahim did not hesitate in sacrificing his precious possessions for the sake of his cause.

When Ibrahim was struggling hard against the forces of evil around him the oppressors conspired to kill him. Then he migrated for the cause of truth and justice. When Isma'il was born and 'reached the age of serious work, with his father, Ibrahim said; "O my son; I see in vision that I offer thee in sacrifice. Now see what is thy view (the son) said: O my father! Do as thou art commanded. Thou will find me, if God so wills, one practising patience and constancy." (37: 97–102).

"Who can be better in (following) a way of life than

one who submits his whole self to God, does good, and follows the way of Ibrahim, the true in faith (*Hanif*)? For God did take Ibrahim for a friend." (4: 125). Ibrahim is the model for those who follow truth and lead pure lives dedicated to the liberation of the oppressed human beings from the slavery of tyrants, masters, lords, and god-kings.

12

YUSUF : THE PROPHET WHO PERSEVERED IN ADVERSITY.

Prophet Ibrahim (Abraham) is the father of the Semitic prophets who lived and worked in the Near East: Egypt, Syria, Palestine, Arabia and Mesopotamia. Prophet Yusuf was the son of Prophet Ya'qub (or Isra'il: the soldier of God). Ya'qub was the son of prophet Ishaq, (Isaac), the son of Ibrahim. Ya'qub(Jacob) had four wives. From three of them he had ten sons. When he became old he had from Rahil (Rechel) two sons Yusuf (Joseph) and Binyamin (Benjamin), the latter was the youngest.

1. The Story of Courage and Fortitude:

Prophet Ya'qub and his twelve sons were shepherds who kept their flocks of sheep, goats and camels in Canaan, in Palestine. He was an old man, a kind-hearted patriarch and leader of his tribe, a righteous man of God. Yusuf was a handsome boy of seventeen years, a truthful, courageous, and sincere boy growing into a noble and righteous man whom his father loved dearly for he was of noble demeanour and pious character. His half-brothers, jealous of his nobility, piety and wisdom hated him and plotted to remove him away from their path.

The story of Yusuf is the story of fortitude, patience and perseverance. He preferred imprisonment to the ignominy of compromising with evil and oppression. He rejected the corrupt ways of his contemporary society and stood alone in his path of truth, rectitude and goodness: "We gave him (Ibrahim), "says the Qur'an, "Ishaq, Ya'qub: all three We guided. And before him We guided Nuh and among his progeny, D'aud, Sulayman, Ayyub, Yusuf, Musa and Harun. Thus do We reward those who do good. And Zakariya and Yahya, 'Isa and Ilyas (were) all in the ranks of the righteous. And Isma'il, Yasa'a, Yunus and Lut: and to all We gave favour above the nations." (6: 84–86).

According to the Qur'an, the story of Yusuf is the most beautiful story of the Qur'an because this reveals the contradictions of life and the contrast between the forces of evil and goodness. Yusuf suffered because of the pettiness, selfishness, lust, greed and jealousy of ordinary human beings. He was the chosen of God, wise, bold and honest who resisted evil with bravery and patience. He gave up the corrupt social order and preferred prison to a life of depravity and lewdness. He bore humiliations, persecutions with calmness and had the courage to forgive his oppressors.

In his boyhood he saw a vision: "Behold, Yusuf said to his father: "O my father; I did see eleven stars and the sun, and the moon: I saw them prostrate themselves to me"! Said (the father): "My dear little son relate not thy vision to thy brothers, lest they concoct a plot against thee; for Satan is to man an avowed enemy." (12: 4-5).

The ten half-brothers at last conspired to remove Yusuf from their way. On some pretext they took him to a desert and threw him into a well in order to starve him to death; they lied to their father that a wolf had killed and devoured Yusuf. Later, they came to the well and sold him to a caravan of travellers for a paltry sum of money. The travellers took him to Egypt where he was sold to 'Aziz, an officer of the Pharaoh. He was seventeen years old at that time. "When Yusuf attained his full manhood, We gave him power and knowledge: thus do We reward those who do right." (12: 22).

The wife of 'Aziz, Potiphar, Zulaykha, tried to seduce Yusuf the handsome slave but he saved himself and did not fall in her evil trap. He, being a slave, could not refuse the bidding of his masters. It appears that the upper society of Egypt was scandalized due to this infamy of the women of high officers who took the disobedience and righteousness of Yusuf to be an effrontery to their pride and prestige. So he was humiliated and put in a prison under the false accusation that he had dared to seduce women of high society whereas the truth was on the contrary. When he was imprisoned, he said: "O my Lord! the prison is more to my liking than that to which they invite me. Unless Thou turn away this snare from me I should (in my youthful folly) feel inclined towards them and join the ranks of the ignorant." (12: 33). "Then it occurred to the men, after they had seen the things, (that it was best) to imprison him for a time." (12: 35).

2. The Imprisonment:

In the prison, he spent his time in prayer and meditation. He preached his mission of truth and equality to the fellow prisoners. This prison was safe from the onslaughts of evil. His struggles against corruption had now started. He had revolted against the evil social order and intrigues of the corrupt rulers:

"I have abandoned the ways of a people that believe not in God (truth and equality), and that (even) deny the Hereafter," he told his fellow prisoners. "And I follow the ways of my fathers, Ibrahim, Ishaq and Yaqub and never could we attribute any partners whatever to God: that (comes) of the grace of God to us and to mankind; yet most men are not grateful. O my two companions of the prison! (I ask you): Are many lords differing among themselves better, or the One God, Supreme and Irresistible? If not Him, ye worship nothing but names which ye have named–ye and your fathers for which God hath sent you no authority: the command is for none but God. He hath commanded that ye worship none but Him: that is the right way of life, but most men understand not. . . "(12: 37–40).

Yusuf revolted against the corrupt ways of the Egyptians and stood alone in his fight against evil, temptation, perfidy, falsehood and lust. He was a slave and an ordinary person but he did not sell his soul and honour for money, power, privilege and luxury of the royal court. He spurned everything. He rejected all temptations and offers of 'high' life of ease and lewdness. He bore his adversities with patience and tolerated humiliations with courage and dignity. He was a man of God and truth and this gave him courage and strength to face the forces of evil which he hated. There cannot be any compromise of truth with falsehood and of goodness with evil. He lingered in the prison for many years: he was a prophet in chains.

There were two other men with Yusuf in the prison. They were former officers of the Pharaoh. One was a butler who was responsible for king's wines and drinks. The other was the king's baker. Both were accused of conspiring against the king. Yusuf correctly interpreted the dreams of his fellow prisoners. He predicted that the butler would be freed and reinstated in his office and that the baker would be hanged. It happened as Yusuf had interpreted. The butler was freed and the baker was hanged on the orders of the Pharaoh..

Now the story takes a dramatic turn. The Pharaoh saw a dream:

> "And the king (of Egypt) said: 'I do see (in a vision) seven fat kine, whom seven lean ones devour–and seven green ears of corn and seven (others) withered. O ye chiefs! expound to me my vision if it be that ye can interpret visions'. They said: 'A confused medley of dreams: and we are not skilled in the interpretation of dreams'." (12: 43-44).

The butler who still remembered the righteous Yusuf and the interpretation of his dream sought the permission of the king to bring Yusuf from the prison so that he could interpret the king's dream. But when the butler met Yusuf in prison the latter refused to be released unless he was exonerated of all the false charges framed against him. Then Zulaykha told the truth: that Yusuf was innocent: "Said the 'Aziz's wife: now is the truth manifest: it was I who sought to seduce him from his (true) self: he is indeed of those who are (ever) true (and virtuous)" (12: 51). "So the king said: Bring him unto me, I will take him specially to serve about my own person. Therefore when he had spoken to him he said: 'Be assured this day thou art, before our own presence, with rank firmly established, and fidelity fully proved." (12: 54). An ordinary person, a stranger from an unknown land, a slave rises to the position of a Chief Minister of Egypt.

Yusuf interpreted the king's vision with wisdom. He predicted and forewarned that, "For seven years shall

> ye diligently sow as is your wont: and the harvests that ye reap, ye shall leave them in the ear,–except a little, of which ye shall eat. Then will come after that (period) seven dreadful (years), which will devour what ye shall have laid by in advance for them,–(all) except a little which ye shall have (specially) guarded. Then will come after that (period) a year in which the people will have abundant water, and in which they will press (wine and oil)." (12: 47–49).

3. Yusuf Becomes the Chief Minister:

Yusuf thus rose from slavery to be a Chief Minister or grand-chamberlain of the Pharaoh when the latter appointed him to this highest civil post in Egypt. He was given authority and control over the agrarian and financial administration of the empire.

He managed these affairs with wisdom and sagacity. He filled up the granaries of the country with grains which were later sold to the foreigners during the famine years which were severe throughout the Near East. "Thus did We give established power to Yusuf in the land," says the Qur'an, "to take possession therein as, when or where he pleased. We bestow of Our mercy on whom We please, and We suffer not, to be lost, the reward for those who do good. But verily the reward of the Hereafter is the best, for those who believe, and are constant in righteousness." (12: 56–57).

A servere famine afflicted Egypt and the neighbouring land of Palestine. But through his wise planning Yusuf stored the empire's granaries with enough food and he started selling grains to the neighbouring lands when demand rose and with it the price of the grains also rose. This enriched the empire. The famine also spread to Canaan where Yusuf's father and his brothers lived and raised their flocks of goats and camels. The ten cruel brothers, who threw Yusuf into the well and then sold him into slavery also came to Egypt to buy corn. Yusuf recognized them but they did not know him:

> "Then came Yusuf's brothers. They entered his presence, and he knew them, but they knew him not. And when he had furnished them forth with provisions (suitable) for them, he said: 'Bring unto me a brother ye have, of the same father as yourselves, (but a different mother). See ye not that I pay out full measure, and that I do provide the best hospitality? Now if ye bring him not to me, ye shall have no measure (of corn) from me, nor shall ye (ever) come near me" (12: 58–60).

Yusuf put their bartered goods (or money) which they had exchanged against Egyptian corn in their saddle bags which they later discovered when they reached Canaan. They implored Ya'qub to send Binyamin with them because the Egyptian Chief Minister, they told their father, was generous to them as he had returned their money/goods back to them. They succeeded in persuading their father and on the next journey Binyamin accompanied them to Egypt. They arrived in Egypt, purchased corn, loaded it on their camels when suddenly they were stopped by the Egyptian police on the suspicion of stealing the chief's precious drinking cup.

Yusuf had intentionally put the cup in Binyamin's saddle-bag. So Binyamin was detained as an apparent punishment for stealing the chief's cup. When they came to their father, he did not believe his selfish sons. How could Binyamin steal? This was another intrigue of his sons, he thought

The old patriarch was deeply grieved over the loss of another beloved son, after Yusuf. The ten sons ridiculed their father for still remembering Yusuf who, the dishonest sons believed, to have perished as a slave in some remote country. "He (Ya'qub) said: I only complain of my distraction and anguish to God, and I know from God that which ye know not. O my sons! go ye and enquire about Yusuf and his brother, and never give up hope of God's truly soothing Mercy. No one despairs of God's soothing Mercy except those who have no faith." (12: 86–87).

The old prophet forgives his selfish sons and shows great patience and fortitude; and like a man of truth wishes them well and asks them not to despair of God's mercy. He asks them to go and search for Yusuf and Binyamin.

The (nine) brothers went to Egypt again and met Yusuf and told them of their misery and distress of their father who was now almost blind. Now Yusuf revealed himself to his brothers. He forgave all their sins and excesses committed against him:

> "(Yusuf) said: 'know ye how ye dealt with Yusuf and his brother, not knowing, (what ye were doing)? They said: 'Art thou indeed Yusuf? He said: 'I am Yusuf and this is my brother. God has indeed been gracious to us (all): behold, he that is righteous and patient–never will God suffer the reward to be lost, of those who do right. They said: By God! Indeed has God preferred thee above us and we certainly have been guilty of sin'. He said: 'This day let no reproach be (cast) on you. God will

forgive you, and He is the Most Merciful of those who mercy." (12: 89–92).

So at last Ya'qub and his sons all were brought to Egypt. They were all honoured and treated generously. Every excess was forgiven. The patience of Ya'qub and forbearance of Yusuf were rewarded. This story is not just a story of certain characters and roles, but it reveals the eternal struggle between goodness and evil, between right and wrong. The foces of evil planned conspiracies and intrigues but truth ultimately triumphed.

The man of truth is always patient, presevering in adversities; he has faith and trust in God and higher values of life. "There is, in their (prophets') stories, instruction for men endued with understanding. It is not a tale invented, but a confirmation of what went before it,– a detailed exposition of all things and a Guide and a Mercy to any such as believe (in truth)". (12: 111).

13

SHU'AYB AND HIS STRUGGLE AGAINST ECONOMIC INJUSTICE.

About five hundred years before Moses liberated the Israelites from slavery of the Egyptians, there lived around the routes between Egypt and Mesopotamia, the people of Madyan. They were largely merchants and engaged in long-distance trade. Their territory extended from the northeast of Sinai Peninsula upto the northern parts of Jordan valley. They were originally an insignificant small tribe but in due course of time their trade flourished and their civilization prospered in the commercial towns which they established along the trade routes. Their population increased tremendously and their power, influence and dominion consolidated.

1. The Two Social Classes:

Increase of power and accumulation of wealth by rising merchants corrupted the social structure. Internal strife, social conflicts, dissensions and schisms divided the Madyan people into two broad antagonistic social groups: those powerful and rich merchants who strated defrauding and exploiting the weaker groups and tribes in economic exchanges, sales and transactions, and those who came to lose all means of production and sources of sustenance and were even deprived of their due shares in the economic system.

Economic power is also a social and political power which tries to command every thing and rule over all. These two warring sects or classes of the Madyan people became poles apart as their interests became antagonistic. The danger of clash between the two classes became imminent. The people moved around a perilous volcano. The weak were defenceless and at the mercy of the brutes who had no compunction or qualms of conscience. The powerful used brute force to deprive others of their due rights and things and committed highway robberies. This had driven the weak and poor to utter misery and ruin.

Prophet Shu'ayb was a noble, kind-hearted, an upright, bold and righteous man who refused to be one of the oppressors and defrauders of the poor people of Madyan. He revolted against the economic fraud, social anarcly and tyranny of the powerful merchants and hoarders. The arrogant and rich mercantile oligarchy of rulers threatened Shu'ayb and his followers extermination, exile, starvation and death if he continued to attack their corrupt system and fraudulent ways of life. He must acquiesce to their evil practices, customs, laws and religious rituals. That is, he must adopt lies, fraud, treachery, injustice and oppression of the weak and poor under the cover of religion and superstition.

These were the ways of their fathers which they would not abandon on the advice of a poor and insignificant teacher like Shu'ayb who did not possess wealth, political power and social prestige like the rich merchants. "To the Madyan people) (We sent) their brother Shu'ayb. Then he said: 'O my people! serve God and fear the Last Day: nor commit evil on the earth with intent to spread corruption". (29: 36). They refused to accept truth, justice and equality and were therefore destroyed like other oppressors of the weak. (29: 40)" To the Madyan people (We sent) Shu'ayb, one of their own brethren" says the Qur'an in another verse,

> "He said: 'O my people! Obey God, ye have no other God but Him. And give not short measure or weight: I see you (rolling) in wealth but I fear for you the penalty of a Day that will compass (you) all round. And O my people! Give just measure and weight, nor withhold from the people the things that are their due. Commit not evil in the land with intent to do mischief'" (11: 84–85).
>
> "And squat not on every road, breathing threats hindering from the path of God those who believe in Him, and seeking in it something crooked: but remember how ye were little and He gave you increase. And hold in your mind's eye what was the end of those who did mischief. And if there is a party among you who believes in the Message with which I have been sent, and a party which does not believe, hold yourselves in patience until God doth decide between us: for He is the best to decide." (7: 86–87).

2. The Cause of Socio-Moral Degeneration:

Shu'ayb saw that the main cause of his people's moral depravity and social degeneration was the economic fraud and injustice. Justice is to reward or give what is due to individuals, groups or classes. It is the highest virtue, the noblest quality which gives every one his due and share. Justice is the *summun bonum,* the supreme moral value of any economic system. Economic injustice is the root-cause of all social evils, corruption and disequilibrium and discord in society.

It appears that the community of the Madyan people was originally a tribal-pastoral community. And if in a simple barter economy, in exchange and sale the merchants give less to the other party(a buyer, consumer, labourer or borrower) than its due share this would be fraud and exploitation, because in an exchange one man's gain is other man's loss. Just exchange is actually an exchange of equivalent goods for equivalent goods, in measure, weight or number. Systematic profit or gain of one party, group or class confers on it powers and command to subject the poor and weak classes to loss, disadvantage and slavery.

The arrogant merchants ridiculed the very idea of economic justice advanced by Shu'ayb. Justice would imply the abolition of those economic and social institutions which were based on injustice, fraud and exploitation and from which flowed the wealth, power, prestige and privileges of the rich, and poverty, misery and destitution of the poor. The rich merchants explained to Shu'ayb and his followers that they had earned thier wealth and power through their hard labour and through the institutions sanctified by their religion, approved by their ancestors, and hallowed by their traditions and customs. And that they had every right to use it in any way they liked, and that they did not want to share their wealth and power with the dispossessed. Economic equality would be unnatural, irreligious and blasphemous:

> "They said: O Shu'ayb does thy (mode of) prayer command thee that we leave off the worship which our fathers practised, or that we leave off doing what we like with our wealth? Truly thou art the one that forbeareth with faults and is right-min-

ded;". They said: O Shu'ayb! Much of what thou sayest we do not understand. In fact among us we see that thou hast no strength. Were it not for thy family, we should have certainly stoned thee (to death). for thou hast among us no great position." (11: 87 and 91).

The erring people who strove hard to acquire wealth, and material goods held in contempt those humble people who followed higher values of life, truth, justice and goodness. Shu'ayb was, in their eyes a weak, and poor person who lacked wealth, and material goods and had no economic power or high social status. The rich merchants were more afraid of Shu'ayb's tribe than his God, the source of the Message he was delivering to them. The courageous teacher replied to their arguments in a humble and noble way:

"He said: O my people! Is then my family of more consideration with you than God? For ye cast Him away behind your backs (with contempt). But verily my Lord encompasseth on all sides all that ye do. And O my people! Do whatever ye can I will do (my part) soon will ye know who it is on whom descends the penalty of ignominy and who is a liar! And watch ye: For I too am watching with you". (11: 92–93).

And as a righteous man of truth and sincerity, he did not want to take any revenge for their hatred for him. He simply wanted their welfare, reformation and betterment. He wanted to purify the society from weakness, sins, crimes and imperfections. He said: "I wish not, in opposition to you, to do that which I forbid you to do, I only desire (your) betterment to the best of my power: and my success (in my task) can only come from God. In Him I trust and unto Him I return. And O my people!

–let not my dissent (from you) cause you to sin, lest ye suffer a fate similar to that of the people of Nuh, or of Hud or of Salih. Nor are the people of Lut far off from you." (11: 88–89).

As every ruling class justifies it's regime of exploitation and oppression of the weak through an ideology, the rich merchants exploited religion and used its rigid cults to cover economic fraud and injustice meted to the poor. They built houses of prayer out of ill-gotten wealth earned in commercial cheating and fraudulent transactions.

They also gave charity ostensibly and hypocritically out of their illegal wealth. When Shu'ayb exposed their 'pious' fraud and sanctimonious hypocrisy and thus uncovered the naked exploitation of the weak, "they, the leaders, the arrogant party among his people said:

> "O Shu'ayb! We shall certainly drive ye out of our city (community)–(thee) and those who believe with thee; or else ye (thou and they) shall have to return to our ways and religion." He said: 'What even though we do detest (them)? We should indeed invent a lie against God, if we returned to your ways after God hath rescued us therefrom; nor could we by any manner or means return thereto unless it be as in the will and Plan of God, our Lord. Our Lord can reach out to the utmost recesses of things by His knowledge. In God is our trust. Our Lord! Decide thou between us and our people in truth, for Thou art the best to decide. The leaders who rejected (truth) among his people, said: 'If ye follow Shu'ayb, be sure then ye are ruined." (7: 88–90).

This was the declaration of war between the two polarized social groups of the exploiters and the exploited. If the rich merchants had practised on the advice of

Shu'ayb they had to part with their wealth and power: and this would have economically ruined them. And the exploited slaves and workers revolted. So Shu'ayb, it apperars from the Quranic verse, migrated to a safe place and organized the oppressed and persecuted tribes, classes and groups into an armed force and declared war against the corrupt rulers:

> "So Shu'ayb left them, saying: O my people! I did indeed convey to you the Message for which I was sent by my Lord: I gave you good counsel, but how shall I lament over a people who refuse to believe." (7: 93).

In the war the oppressors were destroyed: "When Our Decree issued, We saved Shu'ayb and those who believed with him by (special) Mercy from Ourselves. But the (Mighty) Blast did seize the oppressors, and they lay prostrate in their homes by the morning, as if they had never dwelt and flourished there: Ah! Behold! How the Madyan were removed (from sight) as were removed the Thamud." (11: 94–95; 7: 91–92).

These events and tales of past communities and struggles of prophets for truth, justice and equality which the Qur'an illustrates underline the moral lesson that the societies which split up into warring classes of oppressors and oppressed, strong and weak, are unstable societies and are doomed to extinction: "Such were the communities (of oppressors) whose story We relate unto thee(O Muhammad!): there came indeed to them their apostles with clear Signs, but they would not believe what they had rejected before. Thus doth God seal up the hearts of those who reject (truth and equality). Most of them We found not men (true) to their covenant: but most of them We found corrupt." (7: 101–102).

14

MUSA – THE PROPHET WHO LIBERATED SLAVES

1. Slavery and Freedom:

Slavery and freedom are two opposite terms. A free person or a free community enjoys liberty: a free person is an independent human being. He has will and power to act, to decide and to move; he is alive, he can exercise his talents and faculties, powers and capabilities in an unrestrained, natural way. Similarly, free communities have power and will to act, decide and self-govern.

On the contrary, a slave is an oppressed and abject human being, property or possession, chattel or a thing of a powerful master to whom he is coerced to surrender and submit. The slave has neither will nor power; he does not enjoy any personal liberty: he is unable to resist his powerful master. Thus slavery is negation of freedom. So it is tantamount to death. Slave individuals and slave communities and nations have no will and no freedom to act and decide. They have no autonomy to self-govern. Therefore, they are dead in th social and moral senses.

Slavery may be of several types and forms: physical, social, economic or mental-spiritual. In physical slavery the slave is physically dependent on his master for his life. Social slavery is the collective slavery or dependence of a weak social class, group or tribe on a powerful social calss, group or tribe. Slave-owning communities and feudal social orders were based on economic slavery as in a feudal system, serfs, perpetually tied to the land pay allegiance, homage and tribute to their landlords. Economic slavery is actually the economic dependence of a person, a slave, serf, or a worker for his very existence on the owner of the means of production, lands, fields, pastures, mines or factories:

The Israelites were slaves of the Pharaoh, the god-king of Egypt. "The Pharaoh elated himself in the land, "says the Qur'an, "and he broke up its people into classes; oppressing some among them, their sons he slew but kept alive their females. For he was indeed a corrupt person" (28: 4). "He was arrogant (even) among inordinate trasgressors." (44: 31).

Moses or Musa was the courageous man who stood against iniquity and brute force of the Egyptian god-king and boldly faced the concerted attack of corruption and evil. He was a humble shepherd, simple and honest man of truth, love and justice, a great teacher and a great prophet who succeeded in liberating the Israelites from their centuries old bondage.

The Qur'an illustrates the historical facts of Moses' life and mission alongwith similar heroic struggles of other prophet-revolutionaries as a universal struggle between the forces of goodness and evil. Moses led the forces of truth, justice, love and equality whereas the Pharaoh, the arrogant god-king, headed the forces of falsehood, injustice, insolence, arrogance and oppression. And as always is the case, truth ultimately defeated falsehood.

According to the Qur'an, Moses was born to an Israelite slave woman in Egypt where her people laboured in bondage and humiliation. (The Qur'an does not specify the period, perhaps it was about 1600 years before the birth of Jesus Christ). His mother, afraid of the infant's death at the hands of Egyptian police, hid him for a time and then decided to put the child in a box and threw it in the river. The child was picked up by Pharaoh's wife. Moses was thus brought up in Pharaoh's palace. He grew to be a noble, wise and righteous man uncorrupted by the vices of Egyptian life. In a quarrel between an Israelite slave and an Egyptian officer, Moses sided with his kinsman and killed the Egyptian.

The slaves helped him, and to save his life he escaped to the land of the Midianites in the Sinai Peninsula where he settled for a time and married. This was the *Hijra,* the giving up of the old corrupt order and preparation for the struggle of a new social order. Then he received inspiration as a prophet and resolved to liberate his people from the Egyptian slavery. Moses and his brother Aaron (Harun) challenged the might of the Pharaoh and his corrupt social order based on oppression and slavery of the lower social classes. But the Pharaoh and his chiefs were insolent with power and pride. "And Pharaoh incited his people saying:.

> "O my people! Does not the domination of Egypt belong to me, (Witness) these rivers flowing underneath my (palace)? What! See ye not then? Am I not better than this (Moses), who is a contemptible wretch and can scarcely express himself clearly? Then why are not gold bracelets bestowed on him or (why) come (not) with him angels accompanying him in procession? Thus he made fools of his people and they obeyed him: truly were they corrupt people." (43: 51–54).

The Pharaoh and his powerful chiefs ridiculed the very idea that a simple shepherd of lowly origins, weak, poor and humble could defeat the superior forces of Egypt and liberate the slaves. And instead of revolting against the corrupt social order, Moses must submit to the Pharaoh as he had nourished him and educated and civilized him in his palace. The Pharaoh tried to cajole and trick the honest man: "Did we not bring you up as a child among us and didst thou not stay in our midst many years of thy life?" Thus said the Pharaoh suggesting that he was the god-king, the almighty nourisher of human beings and that Moses was a contemptible murderer and an instigator of the slaves. "And thou didst a deed of thine which (thou knowest) thou didst, and thou art an ungrateful (wretch)". Moses attacked this clever trickery of falsehood with his simple truth and frankness. He replied:

> "I did it then, when I was in error so I fled from you (all) when I feared you; but my Lord has (since) invested me with judgement (and wisdom) and appointed me as one of the apostles. And this is the favour with which thou dost reproach me,– that thou hast enslaved the Children of Israel." (26: 20–22).

The god-king and his advisers, priests, ideologues and administrators took this boldness of the rebels as revolt against their oppressive social order with which were tied their wealth, power and privileges. The Pharaoh said: "Leave me to kill Moses; and let him call on his Lord! What I fear is lest he should change your way of life, or lest he should cause mischief to appear in the land." (40: 26). "So they disputed, one with another, over their affair, but they kept their talk secret. They said: "These two are certainly (expert) magicians. Their object is to drive you out from your land with their magic, and to do away with your most cherished institutions." (20: 62–63).

The most cherished institutions which were now in

danger were the false state religion, the cult of god-king, all degenerated economic, social, political and religious institutions and ideas which had divided human beings into slaves and masters, oppressed and oppressors, the dispossessed and the land-owners and the slave-owners.

2. The Ideology of the Slave - Owners:

The god-king also tried the ideological power of magic and propaganda, of the invented false ideas to cast a spell on the mind of Moses and to overawe him like other slaves into illusions and deceptions. The concerted attack of oppressors is sometimes so overwhelming and sudden through the official media and official religion that it gives the false appearance of truth. Untruth and evil are made to appear as truth. Even very bold spirits become afraid of the well-planned onslaught of evil. But the bold and truthful man proclaims his truth with confidence, wisdom and honesty; and truth has power to dissipate the ideological confusion and to destroy all falsehood, as bright sun removes away the mist and darkness from the sky. Ignorance is like the night and revelation, and truth, are like the day.

The Pharaoh, his chiefs, advisers and priests played tricks and planned conspiracy against Moses. "So concert your plan," the Pharaoh ordered his men, "and then assemble in (serried) ranks: he wins (all along) today who gains the upper hand. "They said: 'O Moses! whether wilt thou that thou throw (first) or that we be the first to throw'? He said: 'Nay, throw ye first'? Then behold their ropes and their rods—so it seemed to him on account of their magic—began to be in lively motion. So Moses conceived in his mind a (sort of) fear." (20: 64– 67). . . "So when they threw they bewitched the eyes of the people, and struck terror into them: for they showed a great (feat of) magic." (7: 116).

The social order of oppression and exploitation is ideologically sustained by a systematic propaganda of lies and subterfuge which instills terror in the hearts of the oppressed. With this ideology of falsehood and terror the ruling classes perpetuate their oppression of the weak. The rod of Moses is the symbol of truth, justice and equality. "We put it into Moses' mind by inspiration: 'Throw (now) thy rod': and behold! it swallows up straightway all the falsehoods which they fake! Thus truth was confirmed, and all that they did was made of no effect. So the (great ones) were vanquished there and then, and were made to look small." (7: 117–119; 26: 45). "When they had their throw, Moses said: 'what ye have brought is sorcery: God will surely make it of no effect: for God prospereth not the work of those who spread corruption. And God by His words doth prove and establish His Truth, however much the sinners may hate it." (10: 81–82).

Ropes and rods are metaphorical and allegorical in these verses. The sorcerer's ropes and rods seemed to the people serpents. That is, the clever rulers had craftily, under coercion and compulsion, illusion and deception made the simple people believe in false things, in wrong ideas and corrupt institutions, such as, god-king was the almighty who gave them everything, life and food, honour and bounty and that the system of slavery was a natural system ordained by their gods. They also terrified the people by persecuting and slaying those who disobeyed these rituals and cults.

All this was perpetuated in order to preserve their oppressive social order. But the simple truth declared by Moses, the courageous man, was more powerful; it destroyed their false ideology, removed confusion and mist from peoples' minds. They now saw clearly the truth of Moses' message of human equality. And then the distinctions between right and wrong, true and false, good and bad, light and dark all became discernible, clear and manifest: "We granted to Moses and Aaron, the criterion (for judgement) and a light and a Message for those who would do right." (21: 48).

On regaining will and power, self-confidence and wisdom the slaves stood up under the leadership of courageous Moses, broke off their shackles, and threw away the yoke of social, economic and mental slavery. The slaves became alive and free. The Pharaoh and his cruel and arrogant chiefs and his iniquitous social order was destroyed: "Pharaoh led his people astray instead of leading them on the right path." (20: 79). A corrupt order and a false ideology never endure.

As long as the Israelites observed the principles of truth, equality and justice they remained strong and prospersous but, when they split up into warring groups and classes enslaving and oppressing each other their fate was the same as that of the Pharaoh and his chiefs "Those who break God's Covenant (of truth and justice) after it is ratified, and who sunder what God has ordered to be joined, and spread corruption on earth; these cause loss (only) to themselves. How can ye reject the faith in God (and truth)?– seeing you were without life, and He gave you life. . ." (2: 27–28).

And what was the Covenant? It was to proclaim truth and to establish a just and equalitarian society without slaves and masters, oppressed and oppressors; that is, a free and equal society:

> "And remember We took a Covenant from the children of Israel (to this effect): Obey none but God;

treat with kindness your parents and kindred, and orphans and those in need. Speak fair to the people. Be steadfast in *Salat* and practise *Zakat*. Then did ye turn back, except a few among you, and ye backslide (even now). And remember We took your Covenant (to this effect): shed no blood amongst you, nor turn out your own people from your homes: and this ye solemnly ratified, and to this ye can bear witness. After this it is ye, the same people who slay among yourselves and banish a party of you from their homes: assist (their enemies) against them, in guilt and rancour: and if they come to you as captives, ye ransom them though it was not lawful for you to banish them."(2: 83–85).

According to the Qur'an, oppression and iniquity, falsehood and evil are eventually destroyed by the forces of truth and equality. The Quranic portrayal of Moses' struggle against the powerful slave-owners of Egypt underlines the fact that, although the Quranic perception of class struggle is pre-feudal and pre-capitalist, tinged with theological conceptions, class struggle is a universal phenomenon which transcends all aspects of history.

The story of Moses teaches the lesson that truth always prevails and oppression (*Zulm*) never lasts. "And We made a people, considered weak (and of no account) inheritors of land in both East and West,–lands whereon We sent down Our blessings. The fair promise of thy Lord was fulfilled for the children of Israel, because they had patience and constancy, and We levelled to the ground the great works and fine buildings, which the Pharaoh and his people erected (with such pride)." (7: 137).

15

'ISA – THE PROPHET WHO LED THE WEAK.

"Masih ibn Maryam (Christ* the son of Mary) was no more than an apostle," says the Qur'an, "many were the apostles that passed away before him. His mother was a woman of truth. They both used to eat (their) food." (5: 75–76). "Christ Jesus, the son of Mary, Masih 'Isa ibn Maryam was (no more than) an Apostle of God, and His word, which He bestowed on Maryam, and a spirit proceeding from Him: so believe in God and His apostles. Say not 'Trinity'; desist; it will be better for you: For God is One God. Glory be to Him; (far Exalted is He) above having a son. To Him belong all things in the heavens and on earth. And enough is God as a Disposer of affairs. Christ will not disdain to serve and obey God, nor will the angels, those nearest (to God). Those who disdain His obedience and are arrogant, He will gather them all together unto Himself to (answer)." (4: 171–172).

"That they (i.e. the Jews contemporary of Christ) rejected (truth) and that they uttered against Maryam a great false charge. That they said (in boast) 'we killed Christ Jesus the son of Mary, the Apostle of God';–but

---

* In Greek Christos means the anointed one and *Masih*, in Hebrew and Arabic, has the same connotation. In ancient times kings and high priests were anointed in order to bestow on them consecration and holiness; that is, he is a chosen one of God.

they killed him not, nor crucified him, but so it was made to appear to them, and those who differ therein are full of doubts with no (certain) knowledge, but only conjecture to follow, for of a surety, they killed him not;– nay, God raised him up (i.e. he was honoured as a prophet-revolutionary) unto Himself: and God is Exalted in Power, Wise." (4: 156–158).

This is in brief the Quranic outline of a great prophet-revolutionary 'Isa ibn Maryam, a righteous teacher, a man of truth who revolted against the corruption and exploitation of the oppressors and led the weak and poor against them in the Roman province of Palestine and was arrested and crucified (*circa* A.D. 41-44). He was the son of a saintly woman Maryam (Mary). The exact details of 'Isa's birth, life and death are hidden in mystery as the only sources for studying his life and mission are the New Testament (Evangel or Gospel) and the Qur'an. He lived in Palestine in the time of Roman emperors Augustus and Tiberius. The orthodox Christians believe that he was crucified by the Roman Governor and the high priests after declaring him a rebel agains the corrupt social and economic order and a threat against the religious cults and rituals; and that he died and was buried, and on the third day he rose in the body with the wounds on his body, walked about and took food with his disciples, and was afterwards lifted to heaven in the body.

This belief is the cornerstone of the Christian doctrine of blood sacrifice and vicarious atonement for sins; that is, 'Isa died for the sins of erring humanity. This religious belief is not supported by the Qur'an.

1. The Man of God:

According to the Qur'an, 'Isa was a humble human

being, a prophet-revolutionary, a man of God who trod the straight path of truth like other prophet-revolutionaries. He was a human being, a divinely-inspired teacher, *Ruh Allah,* 'Inspiration of God,' the courageous fighter against evil and oppression. He was not killed or crucified because the prophet-revolutionaries never die. They always live in the heart and conscience of humanity. "Certainly they killed him not, he was rather honoured by God and raised him to Himself". . (4: 157–158). He was an inspired prophet like other prophets: "We have sent thee (O Muhammad!) inspiration as We sent it to Nuh, and the Messengers after him; We sent inspiration to Ibrahim, Isma'il, Ishaq, Ya'qub, and the Tribes, to 'Isa, Ayyub, Yunus, Harun, Sulayman, and to Da'ud We gave the Psalms." (4: 163). "When 'Isa came with Clear Signs, he said: 'Now have I come to you with Wisdom, and in order to make clear to you some of the (points) on which ye dispute; therefore fear God and obey me. For God, He is my Lord and your Lord: so obey ye Him; This is a Straight Path. "(43: 63–64).

'Isa was a prophet-revolutionary who taught to his followers truth and social equality, love and brotherhood: "He ('Isa) said: 'I am indeed a servant of God; He hath given me revelation and made me a prophet. And He hath made me blessed wheresoever I be, and hath enjoined on me *Salat* (prayer) and *Zakat* as long as I live. He hath made me kind to my mother, and not overbearing or miserable (or hard-hearted). So peace is on me the day I was born, the day that I die, and the day that I shall be raised up to life (again). Such was 'Isa ibn Maryam: a man or word of truth about which they (vainly) dispute. . . . " (19: 30–34).

The moral and social degeneration of the Jews has been described by the Qur'an (5: 13–14) as follows:

"God did aforetime take a Covenant from the children of Israel, and We appointed twelve captains among them, and God said: 'I am with you, if ye but establish *Salat* and give *Zakat* and believe in my apostles, honour and assist them, and loan to God a beautiful loan, verily I will wipe out from you your evils (imperfections), and admit you to Gardens with rivers flowing beneath. But if any of you, after this, resisteth faith, he hath truly wandered from the path of rectitude. And because of their breach of their Covenant We cursed them, and made their hearts grow hard. They change the words from their (right) places and forget a good part of the Message that was sent them: . . . . . . (5: 13–14).

In the chapter or Sura Maryam (19), the Qur'an describes the lives and struggles of the prophet-revolutionaries and their relationships with their families and societies in which they lived. Zakariyya was followed by his son Yahya in their fight against evil and falsehood (19: 1–15). Maryam, the mother of 'Isa was maligned and humiliated by her people, but 'Isa was an upright and righteous son who served his mother and protected her (19: 16–40).

Ibrahim was oppressed and persecuted by his people but he left them and migrated for the cause of truth. Musa fought against the Egyptian Pharaoh. Isma'il followed the path of truth shown to him by God. The prophet Idris was also a man of truth. (19: 45–65). All these men of truth were not only great prophet-revolutionaries but followed the path of truth in their personal lives, in their relations with their families, tribes, societies and in day-to-day activities.

For the study of prophet 'Isa's life and works the

four books of the New Testament, called in the Qur'an Gospels or Evangel (Injil) are the Books of St. Matthew, St. Mark, St. Luke and St. John. According to modern scholars, by the end of the second century A.D., these Gospels were in existence.* The life-sketch of 'Isa, Jesus, is, according to the Old Testament as follows:

'Isa (Jesus) was born to Maryam (Mary) in Bethlehem, Judaea, in the days of the king Herod. Fearing the death of their son, at the hands of the rulers, Mary and her husband, Joseph, took him to Egypt. After the death of Herod, the king, they came back to Palestine and settled in Galilee, in the town of Nazareth, from which Jesus was called a Nazarene, and his followers Nazarenes. (Arabic: Nasara).

In those days a prophet-revolutionary, named, John the Baptist (Yahya) was preaching truth, equality and brotherhood to the people who had become inured to evil and false ways of life. "And the same John had his raiment of camel's hair, and a leathern girdle about his loins; and his meat was locusts and wild honey. "St. Matt. 3:4). He was a man of God, a simple, honest and humble leader of the poor. He was arrested and put in a dungeon.

Now Jesus started his preaching. He enjoined upon the people to adopt the path of righteousness, and truth, the straight path of God, shun all evil and falsehood. He preached among the fishermen and the poor people. "And Jesus went about all Galilee, teaching in their synagogues, and preaching the gospel of the kingdom, and healing all manner of sickness and all manner of disease among the people. And his fame went throughout all Syria. . . And there followed him great multitu-

---

*'Abd Allah Yusuf Ali, *The Holy Quran*, I, 286.

des of people from Galilee, and from Decapolis and from Jerusalem and from Judaea, and from beyond Jordan." (St. Matt. 4: 23–25). And seeing the multitudes he went up into a mountain: and when he was set, his disciples came into him. And he opened his mouth, and taught them, saying:

"Blessed *are* the poor in spirit: for their's is the kingdom of heaven. Blessed *are* they that mourn: for they shall be comforted. Blessed *are* the meek: for they shall inherit the earth. Blessed *are* they which do hunger and thirst after righteousness: for they shall be filled. Blessed *are* the merciful: for they shall obtain mercy. Blessed *are* the poor in heart: for they shall see God. Blessed are the peacemakers: for they shall be called the children of God. Blessed *are* they which are persecuted for righteousness' sake: for their's is the kingdom of heaven. Blessed are ye, when *men* shall revile you, and persecute *you* and shall say all manner of evil against you falsely, for my sake. Rejoice, and be exceeding glad: for great *is* your reward in heaven: for so persecuted they the prophets which were before you."(St. Matt. 5: 1–12).

Jesus wandered from place to place, in towns, in villages, deserts and mountains with his multitudes of poor people sermonizing on honest and truthful living, and humility. He argued with priests, disputed with rulers and officials, and addressed scholars in synagogues. He told parables in the simple language of the common people in order to admonish them and warn them of immoral and corrupt ways of life.

2. Hypocrisy of the High Priests:

Jesus attacked the hypocrisy of the Pharisees who followed the outward rituals of the sacred 'Law' and indulged in all kinds of iniquities and evils. He did not observe the 'Law' hypocritically like the Scribes and Pharisees, and cared more about ameliorating the miserable conditions of the poor. This roused the labourers, workers and slaves against the rich and the priests. "Then the Pharisees went out and held a council against him, how they might destroy him." (St. Matt., 12: 14).

Jesus lived in poverty, without storing or hoarding wealth or food: he wandered from place to place thronged by the poor, sick and the downtrodden. He gave them to eat, served them and lived with them as a poor man. He had revolted against the corrupt social order. To a youngman who came to him to seek advice, he told: "If thou wilt be perfect, go *and* sell that thou hast, and give to the poor, and thou shalt have treasure in heaven: and come and follow me."

"But when the youngman heard that saying he went away sorrowful: for he had great possessions. Then said Jesus unto his disciples, verily I say unto you, that a rich man shall hardly enter into the kingdom of heaven. And again I say unto you, It is easier for a camel to go through the eye of a needle, than for a richman to enter into the kingdom of God. When his disciples heard *it,* they were exceedingly amazed, saying, Who then can be saved? But Jesus beheld *them* and said unto them, With men this is impossible; but with God all things are possible. Then answered Peter and said unto him, Behold, we have forsaken all, and followed thee; what shall we have therefore? And Jesus said: unto them, Verily I say unto you, that ye which have followed me, in the regeneration when the Son of man shall sit in the throne of his glory, ye also shall sit upon twelve thrones, judging the twelve tribes of Israel. And everyone that hath forsaken houses or brethren, or sisters or father or mother, or wife, or children or lands, for my name's sake shall receive an hundredfold, and shall inherit everlasting life; But many *that are* first shall be last, and the last *shall be* first." (St. Matt: 19: 21–30).

The rebels who, like Jesus, had revolted against the false social system and hypocritical way of life, had forsaken everything for the sake of a new just society based on truth and equality. The revolutionaries do not revolt only against the corrupt social order in general but they also reject the ways, habits, ideas, customs, passions, desires, selfishness, jealousies, arrogance, pride, avarice, cowardice, the wrong standards of behaviour patterns, thoughts, their hypocrisy, duplicity and their double standards, backbiting, envies, the ills of the general people. "And when he was come into Jerusalem, all the city was moved, saying who is this? And the multitude said. this is Jesus the prophet of Nazareth of Galilee." (St. Matt: 21: 10–11).

"And Jesus went into the temple of God, and cast out all them that sold and bought in the temple and the seats of them that sold doves. And said unto them, It is written, My house shall be called the house of prayer; but ye have made it a den of thieves." (St. Matt: 21: 12–13).

Jesus continued his preaching and at the same time he attacked the hypocrisy of the priests who used religion as a cover under which they exploited the naive masses and oppressed rebellious people who regarded Jesus as a man of truth, a prophet indeed. (St. Matt: 21: 15–46).

The Pharisees at last tried guile and deception in entangling the man of truth: "Then went the Pharisees and took counsel how they might entangle him in *his* talk. And they sent out unto him their disciples with the Herodians, saying. Master we know that thou art true, and teachest the way of God in truth, neither carest thou for any *man*: for thou regardest not the person of men. Tell us therefore, What thinkest thou? Is it lawful to give tribute unto Caesar, or not? "(St: Matt. 21: 15–17).

This was a clever trick and a wile device to show to the government of the day that Jesus was not only a blasphemer of their religion but also a rebel against the social and political system and its ruler, the Roman Emperor. At this time Palestine was a province of the Roman Empire and was ruled by the Roman governor. "But Jesus perceived their wickedness,. and said, Why tempt ye me, *ye* hypocrites? Shew me the tribute money. And they brought unto him a penny. And he saith unto them, Whose is this image and superscription? They say unto him, Caesar's. Then saith he unto them, Render therefore unto Caesar the things which are Caesar's and unto God the things that are God's."(St. Mtt: 22: 18–21).

The main target of the attacks of Jesus were the lawyers and the Pharisees who possessed the religious authority to interpret the laws of Torah. These priests and scholars generally misguided the poor people and did not act on what they preached. They were in collusion with the corrupt rulers. "Then spake Jesus to the multitude, and to his disciples saying, The scribes and the Pharisees sit in Moses' seat. All therefore whatsoever

> they bid you observe, *that* observe and do; but do not ye after their works: for they say, and do not. For they bind heavy burdens and grievous to be borne, and lay *them* on men's shoulders, but they *themselves* will not move them with one of their fingers. But all their works they do for to be seen of men: they make broad their phylacteries, and

enlarge the borders of their garments and love the uppermost rooms at feasts, and the chief seats in the synagogues, and greetings in the market and to be called of men, Rabbi, Rabbi. But be not ye called Rabbi: for one is your Master, *even* Christ: and all ye are brethren. And call no man your father upon the earth: for one is your Father, which is in heaven. . . . But woe unto you, scribes and Pharisees, hypocrites for ye shut up the kingdom of heaven against men: for ye neither go in *yourselves* neither suffer ye them that are entering to go in. Woe unto you, scribes and Pharisees, hypocrites! for ye devour widows' houses, and for a pretence make long prayer: therefore ye shall receive the greater damnation. Woe unto you, scribes and Pharisees, hypocrites! for ye compass sea and land to make one proselyte, and when he is made, ye make him two-fold more the child of hell than yourselves. Woe unto you, ye blind guides, which say, Whosoever shall swear by the temple, it is nothing, but whosoever shall swear by the gold of the temple, he is a debtor! . . Woe unto you, scribes and Pharisees, hypocrites! for ye pay tithe of mint and anise and cummin, and have omitted the weightier *matters* of the law, judgement, mercy, and faith: these ought ye to have done and not to leave the other undone. *Ye* blind guides, which strain at a gnat, and swallow a camel. Woe unto you, scribes and Pharisees, hypocrites! for ye make clean the outside of the cup and of the platter, but within they are full of extortion and excess. *Thou* blind Pharisee, cleanse first that *which is* with in the cup and platter, that the outside of them may be clean also. Woe unto you, scribes and Pharisees, hypocrites! for ye are like unto

> whited sepulchres, which indeed appear beautiful outward, but are within full of dead men's bones, and of all uncleanness. Even so ye also outwardly appear righteous unto men, but within ye are full of hypocrisy and iniquity. . . (St. Matt., 23: 1–28).

Jesus taught people to be honest, clean-hearted, truthful and sincere without any disharmony between heart and mind. Those who became his disciples he made them courageous and selfless men of truth. With his teachings and his exemplary life he used to enthuse 'spirit' and life in the morally 'dead' persons. He made them bold and resolute, and brought life to 'dead' souls. (Qur'an; 3: 49). The poor, the weak, the slaves also followed him. They left their hearths and homes, families and tribes for a new life of truth and equality. The social order and those who ruled over it were menaced by this revolt of the downtrodden. Jesus was arrested. Before his arrest, the oppressors tried to kill him several times but he escaped. And the whole multitude of them arose, and led him unto (Pontius) Pilate, the Roman governor. "And they began to accuse him, syaing, We found this *fellow* perverting the nation, and forbidding to give tribute to Çaesar, saying that he himself is Christ a King." (St. Luke: 23:2). When Pilate found no fault in Jesus and decided to release him the Pharisees, the Cheif priests accused him of rebellion and blasphemy. "And they were the more fierce, saying, He stirreth up the people, teaching throughout all Jewry, beginning from Galilee to this place. (St. Luke: 23:5). "And when they were come to the place which is called Calvary, there they crucified him, and the malefactors, one on the right hand, and the other on the left. Then said Jesus, Father, forgive them: for they know not what they do. And they parted his raiment, and cast lots. And the people stood beholding. And the rulers also with them derided *him*, saying, He saved others, let him save himself, if he be Christ, the chosen of God. And the soldiers also mocked him, coming to him, and offering him vinegar. And saying, If thou be the king of the Jews, save thyself. And a superscription also was written over him in letters of Greek, and Latin, and Hebrew, 'This is the King of the Jews.' (St. Luke: 23: 33–38).

3. The Unarmed Prophet:

So the prophet-revolutionary 'Isa ibn Maryam was crucified. He was humiliated and killed because he did not arm himself and his followers. It appears that he believed in truth, love and brotherhood and hated violence, revenge and destruction. His submission to the Will of God was complete; he was a divinely-inspired prophet-revolutionary, like Ibrahim and Musa, and thus literally, a Muslim. "The submission of Jesus to the will of God, 'even unto the death of the cross' is a major clue to the mystery of his suffering," says Geoffrey Parrinder in his study, *Jesus in the Qur'an*. "The deep Semitic religious attitude of utter self-surrender to the will of God is here. Jesus is the *'abd,* the servant, fully surrendered to God and so truly worshipping him. He is the servant of the servants of God, who came not to be ministered unto but to minister, and to give his life a ransom for many.' He is the suffering Servant, 'despised and rejected of men.' He is the Son of man, the Messiah, truly human, yet exalted, for 'God raised him to himself".*

'Isa fought for truth and social equality and became a martyr for his noble cause. He said: "It is God who is

* Geoferry Parrinder, *Jesus in the Qu'ran* (London: Faber and Faber, 1965), P. 121.

my Lord; then obey Him. This is a Path that is straight. When 'Isa found that they (the corrupt people) had rejected (truth), he said: Who will be my helpers to (the cause of) God?" The Disciples said: We are God's helpers: we believe in God, and do thou bear witness that we are Muslims (surrendering their wholeselves to the will of God). 'Our Lord! we believe in what Thou has revealed, and we follow the apostle; then write us down among those who bear witness.' And then they (the rejecters of truth) plotted and planned and God too planned, and the best of planners is God. Behold! God said: O 'Isa! I will take thee and raise thee to Myself and clear thee (of the falsehood) of those who blaspheme; I will make those who follow thee superior to those who reject (truth), to the Day of Resurrection; then shall ye all return unto Me, and I will judge between you of the matters wherein ye dispute. . " (The Qur'an; 3: 51–55).

The common masses of Palestine lived under various sorts of oppressions. The Romans persecuted and exploited them with the help of the native landlords, slave-owners, rulers, and priests. The masses were groaning under a degenerated religion of Judaism which had become an assortment of lifeless rituals and rigid cults the external performance of which freed the practising Jews of all moral responsibilities to the oppressed masses. The concepts and words of Torah were distorted and misapplied. They were applied on the poor and not on the rich.

For the common people Messiah was the title and symbol of their hope of getting freedom from the oppression of the Romans, lords and priests. Jesus was a prophet-revolutionary and the oppressed masses welcomed him as a man of God, truth and equality, the Messiah who would liberate them from the slavery of so-many oppressors. The Israelites were waiting for the Messiah who would be the son of David and who would restore the lost power, glory and honour of Israel. The poor and the weak expected a radical change in the corrupt social order. This was the reason that Jesus received popular support. The oppressed and the exploited left everything behind and followed the prophet-revolutionary who would establish a just community of love, equality and brotherhood, free from hunger, misery and oppression.

This revolt of the masses under a prophet-revolutionary was considered a threat by the Romans, lords, masters, local rulers and the Jewish priests. If there was a radical change or revolution in the existing social, political, economic and religious relations the Jewish priests, who enjoyed considerable local autonomy under Roman rule, would lose their privileges and power.

Jesus stirred and roused the masses against the oppressors but he could not arm himself and his followers. If the prophets and revolutionaries do not organize them into an armed force they cannot fight against the powerful social classes and groups for the ultimate liberation of the oppressed masses and establishement of a free, and egalitarian society. The Christian religious tradition has interpreted it as the non-violent approach of Jesus who was the preacher of love. But the masses were in revolt: they longed for salvation and emancipation from oppressors,–political, economic and religious. Revolutions which remain unarmed and undefended are crushed by the formidable forces of evil and counter-revolution.

Jesus was a great man of truth. He lived like an ordinary, simple, honest and humble person. He thought for others, lived for others, suffered and died for others. He was of ascetic temperament. He prayed alone in secret, not to be seen by others. (St. Mark; 1:35). "And it came to pass in those days, that he went out into a mountain to pray, and continued all night in prayer to God." (St. Luke; 6:12).

He was a wise man, a great teacher and a learned scholar. He was a self-effacing and self-less teacher of the poor and weak. The Qur'an and Hadith record many aphorisms and sayings of this prophet: "Malik ibn Anas says that he heard a saying of 'Isa ibn Maryam: 'Isa used to say: Do not talk too much without remembering God; this would harden your hearts. And a hardened heart is far removed from God which you perceive not. And do not keep an eye on others' sins as if you are their masters, instead watch your own sins as if you are slaves. People are of two types: some suffer due to their sins and some are forgiven; so seek forgiveness for those who are being tortured and praise God for your being free from chastisements and suffering."*

* Malik, *Muwatta'*. II, p. 252.

16

MUHAMMAD*– THE LAST PROPHET –REVOLUTIONARY.

All prophet-revolutionaries were divinely-inspired human beings who revolted against their contemporary social orders of oppression and iniquity. They were men of truth who strove with might and main for the cause of social equality. Their discovery of truth was the light which shone in darkness and gloom. The truth proclaimed by Musa, 'Isa and Muhammad was the same although the societies in which they lived were different. The Qur'an says:

> "It was We who revealed Torah (the Law) (to Musa): Therein was guidance and light. By its standard have been judged the Jews, by the prophets who surrendered (their selves to the will of God, i.e. to truth and social equality), by the Rabbis and the scholars (of law). For to them was entrusted the protection of God's Book, and they were witnesses thereto. Therefore fear not men, but fear Me, and sell not My Signs for a miserable price. If any do fail to judge by (the light of) what God hath revealed, they are the rejectors (of truth).

---

* *'The Life of the Prophet of God'*, (*Sira Rasul Allah*), by Ibn Hisham, is an excellent account of the life, mission and teachings of Muhammad. The English translation by A. Guillaume (London: Oxford University Press, 1955) is a remarkable contribution.

> We ordained therein for them: life for life, eye for eye, nose for nose, ear for ear, tooth for tooth, and wounds equal for equal. But if any one remits the retaliation by way of charity, it is an act of atonement for himself. And if any fail to judge by (the light of) what God hath revealed, they are the wrong-doers. And in their footsteps We sent 'Isa, the son of Maryam, confirming the Torah that had come before him. We gave him the Injil (Evangel, Gospel), therein was guidance and light and confirmation of Torah that had come before him: a guidance and an admonition to those who fear God. Let the people of the Gospel judge by what God hath revealed therein. If any do fail to judge by (the light of) what God hath revealed, they are those who are corrupt. To thee (O Muhammad!) We sent the scripture (or revelation) in truth, confirming the revelation or scripture that came before it and guarding it in safety: so judge between them by what God hath revealed, and follow not their vain desires, diverging from the truth that hath come to thee. To each among you have We prescribed a Law and an Open Way. If God had so willed He would have made you a single people, but (His plan is) to test you in what He hath given you: so strive as in a race in all virtues. The goal of you all is to God (i.e. the higher values of truth, equality and brotherhood); it is He that will show you the truth of the matters in which ye dispute." (Qur'an : 5: 44–48).

The goal of the prophet-revolutionaries, Musa, 'Isa and Muhammad was the establishment of a human social order based on the higher values of truth, social equality and brotherhood. Although their contemporary societies were different in their fundamental structures, institutions, customs, laws and morals, but the basic aim of the revelations which came to them was to proclaim truth, emancipate the oppressed and bring to them equality and brotherhood.

Their 'way of life,' *shir'a* and 'mode of society', *minhaj,* were different and specific to their own conditions and systems, but they had one thing in common: they struggled for truth and fought against oppression and falsehood; they strove for human equality and brotherhood and destroyed iniquity and injustice, since Musa, 'Isa and Muhammad were men of truth, sincerity and honesty. They were teachers of the proletariat and the downtrodden.

Jesus, the prophet-revolutionary, revolted against the oppressors; "he was no more than an apostle, many were the apostles that passed away before him." (5:78). He was crucified since he did not organize and arm himself and his revolutionary followers who had also rebelled against their iniquitous social order, and evil ways and corrupt institutions.

Almost six hundred years after Jesus' crucifixion in the Roman province of Palestine, Muhammad ibn 'Abd Allah, a poor and humble orphan of Mecca in Arabia, revolted against the combined forces of usurer-merchants, slave-owners and priests. Unlike Jesus, he organized his followers and armed them. He was an armed prophet-revolutionary who protected the revolution made by his proletariat..

Muhammad is the last prophet-revolutionary "who rehearses to you the Signs of God containing clear explanations that he may lead forth those who believe and do righteous deeds from the depths of darkness into light". (65: 11).

1. The Prophet-Revolutionary:

Muhammad (A.D. 570-632), literally the 'praised one,' is the last prophet-revolutionary of the Biblical tradition and first revolutionary of the modern age. He is the last prophet, the divinely-inspired man of truth and wisdom who saw light in his heart and mind at a time when forces of evil and falsehood had darkened the horizon and had sapped minds and hearts of suffering human beings.

He liberated slaves, orphans and women, the poor and weak. His inspired word became a standard for distinguishing right from wrong, true from false and good from evil. His mission was the same as that of other prophets before him: supermacy of truth, human equality and brotherhood.

He is the first revolutionary of the modern age because he clearly saw that the eternal strife between good and evil is actually, in its social and economic form, a class-struggle, a fight between oppressed and oppressors, slaves and masters, exploited and exploiters, serfs and lords, the weak and the powerful. As a revolutionary he armed himself and his followers after his migration from the citadel of corruption and evil. He liberated the oppressed from the ruthless oppression and slavery of the usurer-merchants, hoarders, slave-owners, lords and priests in the pre-feudal tribal and pastoral society of the Hijaz, of the early seventh century.

He discovered truth and expressed reality in a new language under new circumstances. The society in which he lived and moved, thought and worked was different from those of Musa and 'Isa. The social formations had changed from pastoral-tribal to pre-feudal which were neither feudal nor pastoral. Truth dawned on Muhammad's mind in the Meccan milieu which was charged with high commercial and financial activities.

The Qur'an was revealed during a period of twenty-three years, in a life-and-death struggle of the oppressed against the powerful oligarchy of merchants, slave-owners and priests. It is essentially a book of class struggle between god-kings (pharaohs) and prophet-revolutionaries, oppressors and the oppressed. It is a declaration of war against all sorts of oppression (*Zulm*). *Zulm* is falsehood. Truth always triumphs, and communities of oppressors, *Quran Zalima,* never last, says the Qur'an.

Muhammad son of 'Abd Allah son of 'Abd al-Muttalib. was born in Mecca in A.D. 570 in the tribe of Hashim of the clan of Quraysh which was the custodian of the religious sanctuary of Ka'ba in Mecca to which thronged the Arab tribes every year for the commercial, economic, social, religious and cultural activities. He grew to be a pious, wise and righteous man. He led a simple, ordinary and humble life, like that of the slaves, workers and poor people of Mecca who were generally looked down upon by the arrogant slaveowners and merchants of Mecca. In his youth he worked as a shepherd and as a labourer in the trading caravans. He was an honest, courageous and pious man.

The Meccan society was riven with acute social and economic disparity, moral decay and religious dogeneration. Brute force was the law and powerful tribes subdued and enslaved the weak tribes. No one was safe beyond the forbidden precincts of Ka'ba, the *Haram,* the holy territory, where feuds, wars and blood-shedding were forbidden. The hungry orphans, widows, slaves and outcastes gathered in the cities, like Mecca and were exploited by the rich usurers, lords and merchants. The priests misinterpreted the scriptures and applied them on the poor and let free the rich and powerful on bribes.

The plight of women was miserable. They were treated like chattels, nay, like goats and sheep and thus were considered property of the tribal chief. Women and children could not fight in tribal wars and therefore they were not entitled for booty or for inheritance in a deceased person's property and wealth. The society was, more or less, similar to the society of 'Isa in Palestine as regards the general oppression and exploitation of the common masses by the chiefs, lords, priests and rulers, foreign or local. This tribal society existed on the principle of might is right. The powerful carried off his booty.

It is reported that Muhammad received his first revelation, or his call to prophethood, in a cave near the city of Mecca where he used to pray and meditate on the corruption, moral depravity and anarchy rampant around him. The suffering of the poor, the anguish of the oppressed pained him. He used to feed the hungry, help the poor and free the slaves. He sat with the slaves, artisans and poor and mixed with them as if he was one of them. His simplicity and love of the poor brought derision, contempt and amazement from the rich Meccans: "What type of a prophet is this"; so wondered the arrogant chiefs, "who eats food and walks in the markets. Why has not an angel been sent down to him to warn (people) with him? Or why has not a treasure been bestowed on him, or why has he not been an owner of a fruit garden to eat fruits from it? The oppressors used to say: 'you do not follow but a man who has been bewitched." (25: 7–8).

2. The Mercantile Oligarchy:

The rich merchants, slave-owners and landlords who were proud of their wealth and material possessions believed that revelation was like political and economic power and it could come only to a rich man, merchant, chief, a high priest or a landlord, and not to an ordinary and humble person who was an orphan and of low and insignificant social origins. "When the Truth came to them (the Meccans) they said: 'This is sorcery and we do reject it'. They said : 'Why is not this Qur'an sent down to some (rich) man in either of the two chief cities (Mecca and Ta'if)"? (43–31). In Mecca were the commercial houses, exchange booths, and trade centres of the rich usurer-merchants and in Ta'if they owned fruit gardens, palaces and summer resorts.

The Meccan oligarchy of exploiters was surprised to see a poor and simple man, an orphan who looked like a worker or a slave, as a revolutionary and prophet. They expected a rich man or a wise priest from among themselves to lead them and do marvellous and miraculous things. They considered him a liar. They said to the prophet-revolutionary:

> "We shall not believe in you until you cause a spring to gush forth for us from the earth. Or you have a garden of date trees and vines; and cause rivers to gush forth in them thus giving abundant water (to the barren land.) Or you cause the sky to fall in pieces, as you claim that it will happen against us: or you bring God and the angels before us, face to face. Or you have a house made of gold, or you ascend a ladder right into the skies. No, we shall not even believe in your ascent untill you send down to us a book which we could read.' Say Glory to my

> Lord. Am I not simply a man, an apostle? (17: 90–93).

The standards of judging right from wrong and true from false were different with the revolutionaries and the oppressors. The former believed in truth, social equality, brotherhood, love, selflessness and humility. The latter hankered after wealth, glitter and brute force and believed in falsehood, inquality, oppression of the weak, hatred, arrogance, selfish desires and lusts. The prophet-revolutionary and his followers had forsaken greed and lust and every thing belonging to the old corrupt order. For them strength lay in truth, simplicity and humility, and not in material possessions and arrogance.

For the usurer-merchants, power resided in wealth, fraud, cunningness, lies and selfishness, and therefore humility was a weakness and selflessness deception, and truth ignominy, equality feebleness and lack of wealth, poverty and destitution. Thus moral scales were reversed. They had lost inner purity and real wisdom to judge right from wrong, good from bad, true from false and just from unjust. This was moral darkness and social confusion and anarchy.

The prophet-revolutionary therefore appeared to the power-hungry and selfish chiefs as a madman possessed of demons, a sorcerer, soothsayer or at the most a poet or a rabble-rouser without any cause who stirred slaves and sympathised with the downtrodden. They even accused him of being an agent taught by some dubious persons: "But those who rejected (truth) said, 'This is nothing but a lie which he has forged, and others have helped him at it." (25: 4; 38: 4–7). "Yet they turn away from him saying: he is taught (by others), a man possessed" (44: 14). "Do they not reflect? Their companion is not seized with madness; he is but a perspicuous warner". (7: 184). "Therefore proclaim thou the praises (of thy Lord): for by the grace of the Lord, thou art no soothsayer, nor art thou one possessed. Or do they say: "a poet: We await for him some calamity (hatched) by time." (52: 29–30).

But Muhammad was a divinely-inspired prophet-revolutionary, on the right path of truth. He followed the way of life, *Milla,* of prophet Ibrahim: like him he submitted his wholeself to the will of God; he conformed to the principles of truth, justice and equality. Like Ibrahim, he stood on the side of the oppressed and the poor, the slaves and artisans. Like Ibrahim, he feared none but God, was resolute, courageous and brave, humble and simple, honest and truthful:

> "Say: verily, my Lord hath guided me to a way that is straight,–the right way of life,–the path trod by Ibrahim, the man of truth and he (certainly) joined not gods with God. Say: Truly, my prayer (communion with the Creator) and my devotion, my life and my death are (all) for God, the Cherisher of the worlds. No partner hath He: This am I commanded, and I am the first of those who bow to His will. Say: shall I seek for (my) cherisher other than God when He is the Cherisher of all things (that exist)?" (6: 161–164).

3. The Early Converts:

The great prophet-revolutionary Ibrahim was the model for Muhammad and his followers. The first converts to the egalitarian movement of Islam are called by the Qur'an as *aradhil* (inferior, wretched, pariah) and *mustad'afun* (the weak and exploited ones). They were mainly the hungry slaves, serfs, workers, artisans, clients, (nominally free slaves), women, and orphans who were of low social origins and status in the social hierarchy of the Hijaz. The rich merchants, tribal chiefs, lords and priests were threatened when their slaves, workers, servants and women started embracing Islam which, in social terms, meant a break with the prevalent social order, and a rebellion against their institutions, religious cults, rituals and customs, depraved morals and chaotic laws. They gathered round the prophet and were emerging as a formidable force of truth, social equality and brotherhood. The oppressors asked the prophet to disband the poor from his fold. But he refused to deliver them to the rich people.

The prophet was himself a poor man, and an orphan whose father had left no property, no garden, slave, animals, dinars or dirhams. "Did not He (God) find thee an orphan and give thee shelter (and care)?, "says the Qur'an to the prophet when he started his revolutionary struggle for truth and equality. "And He found thee wandering and He gave thee guidance. And he found thee in need, and made thee independent. Therefore treat not the orphan with harshness, nor repulse the one who asks for some need, and always keep in mind and proclaim the bounty of thy Lord." (93: 6–11).

Any social revolution is a radical change in the social structure; it is a transformation of the old order into a new order. For the revolutionaries it is a bargain of the new order with the old order; that is, they give up everything belonging to the old dead order and sacrifice their lives, wealth and possessions to achieve their objective: the setting up of a new order of truth, human equality and brotherhood.

The revolutionaries dedicate their lives to truth and equality and their reward is their freedom and emancpation from the slavery of the old immoral order. "God hath purchased of the believers their persons and their goods; for theirs (in return) is the Garden. . . ." (9: 111; see also 2: 153–157).

The revolutionaries fight for the cause of God: to liberate the oppressed and the weak and to establish an order of truth, justice and equality: "And why should ye not fight in the cause of God and of those who being weak are oppressed? men, women and children whose cry is Our Lord! Rescue us from this town whose people are oppressors; and raise for us from Thee one who will protect; and raise for us from Thee one who will help?' (4: 75).

4. Jihad, Zakat and Salat:

The prophet-revolutionary Muhammad and his followers were humiliated and persecuted because they were menacing the social order of corruption and oppression. Consequently the Prophet left Mecca with his followers and came to Yathrib, an agricultural town about two hundred miles to the north of Mecca lying on the trade route to Syria and Egypt.

After their *Hijra,* Migration, in A.D. 622, war (*Jihad*) became inevitable. The oppressors of Mecca were using all resources to destroy this community of truth and equality at Yathrib (or Medina). The revolution had to be armed and defended. Many wars ensued and the Muslim community gradually grew to be strong and consolidated. After the capture of Mecca in A.D. 630 the community greatly expanded.

The prophet-revolutionary founded an egalitarian social order in which basic means of production were held in common and used by all collectively because a community based on truth and equality does not believe in private property of those resources on which people depend for their life and for the basic needs, like, land, water, orchards, mines etc.

Zakat, literally purification, was originally a revolutionary principle according to which the wealth (food, cattle, grains, fruits, clothes etc) surplus to one's basic needs was given to those who lacked them (Qur'an; 2: 219). The pre-feudal community of equals established by the Muslim revolutionaries was a scarcity ridden community where there was not enough for everybody to eat and wear. Therefore, whatever they had, they shared it in common in the Brotherhood of Equality.

The masses were hungry and in tatters, without homes and hearths. Under such circumstances private property could not flourish, and revolutionaries, whether modern or medieval, as a general principle, do not have private possessions in exclusion to other people. The prophet after his death, did not leave any private property, land, garden, well, slaves, cattle, or money. Nor did his followers, who emulated him, leave any property.

Similarly *salat* (prayer), *Hijra*, migration, *Jihad,* war, *amal-i-salih,* the righteous act, were the revolutionary principles of fighting against the forces of oppression and evil. Every act, according to the Qur'an, which aids in emancipating the weak and oppressed and promotes the cause of God is a righteous act (9: 119–129). They were means for some higher purposes and were not ends in themselves. They were not rigid rituals as they became later under feudal times.

To promote social equality and human brotherhood Muhammad, by his precepts, encouraged emancipation of slaves. The early converts of Islam were mainly slaves, artisans, clients (*mawali*: freed slaves), women and orphans. Many of his companions were thus former slaves. Bilal, the African, Suhayb, the Roman, Salman, the Persian, Zayd ibn Haritha, 'Abd Allah ibn Mas'ud, and 'Ammar ibn Yasir were all slaves who rose to eminence after the Islamic revolution.

It has often been asked whether Muhammad did really abolish slavery by an explicit decree? As a prophet-revolutionary, Muhammad believed in human equality and brotherhood. Every revolutionary is a brother unto another revolutionary: without equality no revolution can succed in liberating the oppressed social classes. But Islamic revolution irrupted in a pre-feudal social milieu where slavery was deep-rooted.

The Qur'an exhorted the early Muslim revolutionaries to free their slaves and accept them in the Islamic Bro-brotherhood of Equality: "But he (man) hath made no haste on the path that is steep, and what will explain to thee the path that is steep? (It is:) freeing the slave; or the giving of food in a day of privation to the orphan with claims of relationships, or to the indigent (down) in the dust. . . (90: 11–16).

It was a slave-owning society. Slavery could not be abolished with a single decree or fiat. Many punishments prescribed in the Qur'an also include freeing of slaves and feeding of the hungry and clothing of the poor: "God will not call you to account for what is futile in your oaths, but He will call you to account for your deliberate oaths: for expiation, feed ten indigent persons, on a scale of the average for the food of your families; or clothe them or give a slave his freedom. If that is beyond your means, fast for three days. . . " (5: 89).

Muhammad, the prophet-revolutionary, is the model of a beautiful moral character, *Uswa Hasana* (33:21); he was of an exalted standard of character, *Khuluq 'azim'*

(68:4), 'who would lead forth those who believe and do righteous deeds, from darkness to light.' (65:11). The Qur'an exemplifies the character and life which Muhammad lived. The prophet first revives himself, then he revives the 'dead' society, since moral death is like physical death. An early Meccan *Sura* reads as follows:

> "*Nun:* By the Pen and by the (Record) which (men) write–thou art not by the grace of thy Lord, mad or possessed; nay, verily for thee is a Reward unfailing. And thou (standest) on an exalted standard of character. Soon will thou see and they will see, which of you is afflicted with madness. Verily it is thy Lord that knowest best which (among men) hath strayed from His Path. And He knoweth best those who receive (true) Guidance. So hearken not to those who deny (the truth). Their desire is that thou shouldst be pliant so would they be pliant. Heed not the type of despicable man,–ready with oaths, a slanderer, going about with calumnies, (habitually) hindring (all) good, transgressing beyond bounds, deep in sin, violent (and cruel),–with all that, base-born,–because he possesses wealth and sons. When to him are rehearsed Our Signs, "Tales of the Ancients," he cries. . ." (68: 1–15).

The prophet-revolutionary leads his followers from darkness to light, and to a paradise of truth, equality, love and honesty:

> "For God hath indeed sent down to you (O ye men of understanding!) a Message, an apostle, who rehearses to you the signs of God containing clear explanations, that He may lead forth those who believe and do righteous deeds from the depths of darkness into light."

It is He who has sent His apostle with guidance and the way of life of Truth, that he may proclaim it over all ways of life, even though the pagans may detest it." (61: 9).

And the true 'way of life,' according to the Qur'an is Islam, that is, the proclamation of truth, social equality, the higher values which flow from the Divine source and for which the men of God, prophets and revolutionaries struggle.

4. The Quranic Concept of Islam:

Islam is the 'way of life' (*milla, din*), the mission and aim of the struggles of all prophet-revolutionaries. The Qur'an calls Ibrahim, Musa, 'Isa and Muhammad and their fellow-revolutionries as *Mûslims.* But what is Islam? What are its revolutionary principles and ends? The higher values for which the prophet-revolutionaries fight are(1) supremacy of truth(2) emancipation of the weak and oppressed and(3) establishment of a human community or society based on social equality, love, justice and brotherhood.

For the realization of these values or principles (truth, social equality) the prophet-revolutionaries wage incessant war (*Jihad*) and leave their hearths and homes, familites, tribes, and the old social order for a new egalitarian social order. Those revolutionaries who follow truth and social equality as the ruling principles are called *Muslimun*: and those who reject truth and social equality and deny sincerity, faithfulness, and repudiate justice are called *Kafirun*, or rejecters. The rejecters are the oppressors of the poor. They are liars, and suppressors of truth. They run after false appearances, desires, lusts, pride, arrogance and superstitions.

The *Muslimun* are those who speak the truth in their personal lives, and establish truth in their collective life, i.e. they set up societies based on equality and brotherhood. The *Muslimun* are sincere, honest, faithful, true, courageous, just, selfless, innocent, without hypocrisy and without lusts and selfishness. They are patient, constant, forbearing and persevering. They are true in word, thought and deed.

Literally Islam is submission or surrender of one's whole self to the Will and Plan of God or to the 'Pleasure' or Countenance, of God. It is conformity to truth, sincerity, justice and equality by those who surrender their wills and selves, their desires and aims to the higher Will and Plan of God who is Truth and the only Reality. One who submits to the Will of God, and does whatever pleases Him, he acts in conformity to truth and in agreement with Reality. Islam is faithful adherence to natural laws. Islam is the Way of life of truth, innocence, purity, sincerity, honesty, justice and equality, freedom and fraternity.

5. The Revolutionary Idea:

Islam constitutes the principles of truth and social equality. Opposite of Islam is untruth and iniquity which is denial of truth, rejection of equality and repudiation (*Kufr*) of goodness. Therefore, those who reject truth and social equality are called by the Qur'an *Kafirun*. *Muslimun* and Kafirun are thus opposite to each other. For the Muslimun, the higher values for organizing a just community are truth and social equality which are subsumed by the Qur'an under the two broad principles of *Salat* and *Zakat*. *Salat* is the constant remembrance of God; that is, the values of truth, honesty and sincerity, purity and goodness. The purpose of this remembrance and recollection is the inculcation of these values in the mind of the believer. From this higher principle flows the other principle of *Zakat* which is common sharing or ownership of social means of production to ensure a perfect social equality among the members of the community.

The Qur'an describes the Muslim men and Muslim women in the following words: "God has prepared forgiveness and great reward for men and women who submit (their wills to the will of God) and those men and women who believe (in truth), and men and women who are devout, for men and women who speak the truth, are patient and constant, who humble themselve, who give away (their wealth to the needy brothers and sisters) who fast and (deny themselves), who guard their chastity and who engage much in God's praise." (33: 35). "Whatever ye are given (here) is (but) a convenience of this life but that which is with God is better and more lasting. It is for those who believe and put their trust in their Lord. Those who avoid the greater crimes and shameful deeds and when they are angry even then forgive. Those who hearken to their Lord and establish *Salat*, who (conduct) their affairs by mutual consultation; who spend out of what We bestow on them for sustenance; and those who when an oppressive wrong is inflicted on them, (are not cowed but) help and defend themselves." (42: 36–39). "By the Time, verily man is in loss except those who believe (in truth) and do good deeds and (join together) in the mutual teaching of Truth and of patience and constancy." (103: 1–3).

In another verse the Qur'an clearly says that those Muslim revolutionaries were righteous only who spoke the truth, shared their wealth and substance with the needy, were sincere and patient in adversity and war. (2: 177).

When the Arab Jews and Christians rejected the prophet-revolutionary Muhammad and his message of truth and social equality they ridiculed him and said that felicity and blessedness belonged to them only, the Qur'an gave a broad definition of a Muslim: "And they say: None shall enter paradise unless he be a Jew or a Christian. Those are their (vain) desires or wishful thinking. Say: produce your proof if ye are truthful. Nay–*whoever submits his whole self to God and is a doer of good,* he will get his reward with his Lord: on such shall be no fear nor shall they grieve. (2: 111–112; 31: 22). "When his Lord said to him (Ibrahim): 'Bow (thy will to Me)': He said: 'I bow (my will) to the Lord and Cherisher of the universe. And this was the legacy that Ibrahim left to his sons, and so did Ya'qub: O my sons! God hath chosen the 'way of life' for you; then die not except in the 'way of life' of submitting yourselves (to the Will of God.") (2: 131–132).

The 'way of life' of Ibrahim was truth. "Ibrahim was indeed a model, devoutly obedient to God, (and) true in faith and he joined not gods with God. He showed his gratitude for the favours of God, who chose him and guided him to a straight path." (16: 120–121). "Ibrahim was neither a Jew nor yet a Christian: but he was true in faith and bowed his will to God's ('Muslim'). And he joined not gods with God." (3: 67).

The prophet-revolutionary Muhammad, like the other prophets surrendered himself to the Will of God: which means that he was man of truth. He proclaimed truth and struggled for social equality. He was devoted to his cause. He was a *muslim* by definition, as were all the prophet-revolutionaries. He was a follower of Ibrahim who was a model of truth:

> "Say (O Muhammad!), verily my God hath guided me to a way that is straight, a way of life that is right, the path (trod) by Ibrahim, the ture in faith, and he (certainly) joined not gods with God. Say, truly my *salat* and my devotion, my life and my death are (all) for God, the Cherisher of the worlds. No partner hath he. This am I commanded, and I am the first of those who bow to His will (6: 161–163).

What is the meaning of surrendering one's will to the will of God? This is an exchange, and a bargain in which the revolutionary, according to the Qur'an, surrenders his will to God's. God takes his will, soul, heart, power, talents, mind, his wealth, goods, everything he possesses and bestows on him in return everlasting felictity. He struggles for the cause of truth and equality and thus works for the will of God. In this bargain the revolutionaries, the *muslims* give up the old social order, its wealth, privileges and relations, and struggle for a new social order, a paradise of truth, equality and brotherhood, justice and love. (9: 111). The revolutionaries give their wholeselves and possessions to God; that is, to the cause of truth, and God gives them salvation and freedom from slavery, oppression, falsehood and evil. These Muslims who fight for truth and goodness and are clearly described by the Qur'an as those "who turn (to God) in repentance: that serve Him and praise Him; that wander in devotion to the cause of God (truth); that bow down and prostrate themselves (in humility) in prayer; who enjoin good and forbid evil; and observe the limits set by God; (These do rejoice for the bargain). So proclaim the glad tidings to the believers (in truth) (9: 112). (Also 23: 1–11).

From all these verses of the Qur'an we may conclude that a prophet-revolutionary, Ibrahim, Musa or Muhammad, who surrenders his will, soul, mind, heart, his power, talents, everything which belongs to him to the Divine will is fundamentally a revolutionary who devotes his life and power for truth and social equality.

Truth is a wide term which includes goodness, sincerity, innocence, conformity to laws of nature, social equality, love, brotherhood, honesty and justice. In social terms therefore Islam means a social order which is based on these higher values which make human society a paradise on earth where man does not oppress and exploit another man and where all are equal all are free and all are brothers unto each other. So Islam is in broad terms a system of egalitarianism and truth. This is the Quranic conception of Islam.

7. The Feudalist and Capitalist Conceptions of Islam:

According to the Qur'an, Islam is originally a system or order of truth and social equality. The prophet-revolutionaries struggled for those values and principles throughout their lives. *Salat* and *Zakat* were the two fundamental rules or principles from which all other moral values or laws were derived.

As we shall discuss it in details in the next chapter, *Salat* denoted remembrance or recall of the higher source of all morality, divine or natural which inculcates in the personality of the revolutionary the love of truth, honesty and sincerity, selflessness and faithfulness. And *Zakat* underlined sharing of community's economic resources, means of production, sustenance and enjoyment by all to ensure social and economic equality. *Salat* and *Zakat* are therefore synonymous with truth and social equality.

All prophet-revolutionaries enjoined upon their followers both *salat* and *Zakat*. "Also mention in this Book (the story of) Isma'il: He was (strictly) true to what he promised and he was an apostle (and) a prophet. He used to enjoin on his people *Salat* and *Zakat* and he was most acceptable in the sight of his Lord." (19: 54–55).

All prophet-revolutionaries were men of truth and sincerity. Their *salat* was the truth and their *Zakat* was social equality and justice. And according to the Qur'an the essence of Divine Commands is truth and justice: "The Word of thy Lord doth find its fulfilment in truth and in justice. None can change His words, for He is the one who heareth and knoweth all." (6: 115).

This means that to speak the truth, to struggle for the emancipation of the poor, to wage war against the oppressors and slave-owners and to establish social equality and justice are the real elements of *salat* and constitute righteous acts. One who speaks the truth is acting righteously, in doing this he performs his *salat*. One who fights for justice and social equality, acts righteously and in doing this he performs his *salat*. These are virtuous and righteous deeds, *a'mal saliha.*

As we shall explain soon, *Salat* was not a rigid ritual or a formalistic cult without substance. Likewise the righteous acts of *Jihad*, war, fasting etc, were the means to make the revolutionaries physically strong, patient, resolute and persevering. *Salat* was to make them truthful, sincere and faithful. All these were not ends but means or revolutionary principles for establishing justice and social equality. The real principles or pillars were truth, social equality, struggle (against oppressors), courage and boldness, humility, love, and brotherhood.

Similarly *Zakat* was an equalizing principle, of taking wealth surplus over the basic needs of the rich and then handing it over to those who lacked it, bacause all wealth, economic resources and means of production were to be shared by all for the enjoyment and equal development of all. Through this equalization society could he purified of all imperfections, defects, rivalries, jealousies, strife and antagonism between the rich and the poor social classes. *Zakat* is an act of purification, i.e. freedom from inequality, injustice, oppression, exploitation, selfishness, and acquisitive motives.

After the civil wars and counter-revolution of the Umayyads the revolutionary principles of *Salat, Jihad, Zakat* etc, were all re-interpreted in a feudal framework. Feudalism reasserted when under monarchy and autocracy feudal social and economic relationships of master and slave, lord and serf, king and his subjects replaced the pristine revolutionary principles of justice and social equality. The Qur'anic Islam is the sum of the revolutionary principles of truth and social equality, honesty, sincerity, love and brotherhood, but feudal Islam was a political instrument to enslave the broad massess in the name of pristine Islam.

So *Salat* and *Zakat* gradually lost their moral substances of truth and social equality and became mere rituals and lifeless cults vegetating under feudal slavery and oppression. Under feudalsim, Islam became a rigid ritual, and *salat* became a formalistic cult external performance of which was supposed to absolve the performer of all social responsibility, truth and courage. It was enough to pray several times and speaking of truth, sincerity, equality, Justice and brotherhood were considered unimportant and valueless. This feudal morality, nay immorality, divested the feudal society of all higher values and made society a jungle where brute force reigned and slavery and oppression became the rules. Feudal

Islam was thus a negation of the Quranic Islam, the Islam of the prophet-revolutionaries, the Islam which was synonymous with truth, justice, social equality, sincerity, innocence, humility, love and brotherhood.

Capitalism exploits religion, that is, the decayed Islam and its revolutionary concepts of *salat, zakat, Jihad* etc. as political instruments to suppress the poor working classes and masses, by dividing society into those who own all the major means of production and control all political, social and cultural processes, and those who sell their labour-power. This regime of inequality and oppression is justified on the grounds of a decayed religion which has confined itself to an assortment of shallow rituals devoid of their original moral ethos.

The result is a wholesale justification of inequality, oppression and superstitious rituals which are clearly opposite to the real teachings of the Qur'an and the prophet-revolutionaries. Whereas Islam of the prophet-revolutionaries was the way of truth, enlightenment, social equality, justice and brotherhood, the feudal and capitalist Islam has become the way of untruth, hypocrisy, fraud, iniquity, oppression, slavery, superstition and darkness.

The major principles of capitalism are: profi-motive, ownership of the basic means of production by private capitalists, free market-economy i.e. making everything a commodity to be sold and purchased in the market. This system divides people into broad classes of powerful capitalists and poor preletariat. Capitalism makes people selfish who hanker for profit and run to acquire the power and command of money which makes the rich arrogant and selfish. Capitalism inculcates those lusts and desires and passions which the Quranic Islam discourages. The Quranic Islam enjoins truth, justice and social equality, sincerity and selflessness but capitalism nurtures their opposites. This means that capitalism is opposite to the principles of the Quranic Islam, the principles and values for which the prophet-revolutionaries fought throughout their lives. Capitalist societies are therefore modern societies of oppressors, *Qura Zalima* which oppress the working classes and masses.

The pillars (*arkan*) of Islam were not the rituals or external and formalistic cults of 'prayer,' fasting, payment of alms etc. but truth, justice, social equality, eternal war against oppression and exploitation, and establishment of an equalitarian society. An equalitarian society of educated, refined, civilized and truthful people would be an 'Islamic' society according to the Qur'an and an unequal divided society of illiterate, fraudulent, ignorant, treacherous, insincere, hypocritical and selfish people would be an unislamic or *Kafir,* society according to the Qur'an.

If modern socialism could create an equalitarian society of educated, courageous, honest and sincere people and a social and economic order of justice and perfect social equality it would be closer to the Quranic conception of Islam. There is nothing in a name. A tree is known by the frutit it bears and a social system is known and valued by the quality and character it creates in its members. Individuals are the products of their societies. Dishonest and morally diseased individuals are the creation of dishonest and morally diseased societies.

8. Islam is a Way of Life.

According to the Qur'an, Islam is a way of life, *din,* of all the prophet-revolutionaries and their followers:

The 'way of life' has He established for you as

that which He enjoined on Nuh–that which We have sent by inspiration to thee (O Muhammad!)– and that which We enjoined on Ibrahim, Musa and 'Isa; namely, that ye should remain steadfast in establishing (this) 'way of life' and make no divisions in it. To those who worship other things than God (truth and equality), hard is the way. God chooses to Himself those whom He pleases and guides to Himself those who turn to Him (42: 13).

The 'way of life,' *din,* of all the prophet-revolutionaries was the same in essence. Their fundamental principles and ideals were the same: truth and social equlity for which they waged wars against oppression and evil. These were the principles for which Nuh, Ibrahim, Musa, 'Isa and Muhammad struggled. Truth and equality, brotherhood and love are inconsistent with selfishness, greed, suppression of the weak and falsehood:

> "This day have those who reject (truth) given up all hope of your way of life. Yet fear them not but fear Me. This day have I perfected your way of life for you, completed My favour upon you, and have chosen for you Islam as your way of life"(5: 3).

This verse refers to the Muslim community when it became established as a community of truth and brotherhood in Medina. As long as Muslims were a persecuted community of rebels in Mecca they could not organize and arm themselves as revolutionaries to proclaim and defend their high principles for which they stood and for which they had sacrificed everything.

When they organized themselves as an armed community of equals with their own rules of conduct and liberated themselves from the slavery of the Meccan oligarchy of merchants, usurers, priests and lords they could not be eliminated. They were the believers in truth and equality. They spoke the truth, they were honest and sincere. Whatever they believed or said they acted upon it. They treated each other as equals. They formed a Brotherhood of truth and equality.

This does not mean that all social and economic concepts, institutions, rules and principles evolved by the Muslim revoltutionaries in their long struggle of twenty-three years have been fixed and rigidified into social and economic relations for ever. This cannot be because any human society is a growing organism: it grows and changes. What the verse means is that the Muslim revolutionaries have now founded a community in Medina to practise their values of truth, social equality, justice and brotherhood. These moral values had to be implemented through laws, rules, directives and institutions. What was important was the values and principles and not the institutions which only expressed, reflected and represented the essential principles. Social equality was a principle which was implemented through the institution of *Zakat*.

The principles of truth, social equality and brotherhood are the natural principles which formed the essence of the message of the prophet-revolutionaries. Harmony of nature, cosmos and order of universe and purity of unsullied human conscience and nature, like the innocense of a child, is the natural and spontaneous 'way of life' guided by divine forces: "Nay, the oppressors (merely) follow their own lusts, being devoid of knowledge. But who will guide those whom God leaves astray? To them there will be no helpers. So set thou thy face steadily to the 'way of life' of truth, according to the pattern of pure nature on which God has created mankind. No change (left there be) in the work (wrought). By God! that is the right way of life but most among mankind understand not." (30: 30).

The Quranic concept of *din* as a way of life of truth and social equality is a progressive and dynamic concept. The actual economic and social institutions as social relations may change from one social formation to another but the ideals of truth, justice and equality will always be there. For the prophet-revolutionaries, Ibrahim and Musa, the ideal of social equality was materialized by emancipating the slaves and making them free and equal to each other, but in a capitalist society, as there is now no slavery, the emancipation of the working classes from their economic dependence on capital would be a just action on the part of modern revolutionaries.

This shows that all the heritage of feudal and medieval times in the form of a decayed religion (of Islam) with all its rotten mass of religious institutions, ideologies, classes and groups of vested interests is an anachronism and, strictly speaking, an anathema to the Quranic concept of Islam as a way of life of truth and social equality. What goes under the name of Islam today is nothing but a hypocritical facade of a political nature to cover the brutal exploitation of the broad nasses of the third-word Muslim societies.

Islam is a religious/theological conception which means surrender of human will or plan to the higher Divine Will or Plan. It is not a social system of a certain given society. Islam connotes obedience to certain higher principles of truth, social equality, goodness, brotherhood, honesty, sincerity and love etc. the principles on which a community of equal and free individuals can be founded. The principles were the ideals of all prophet-revolutionaries throughout ancient times. However, the social institutions which were set up within the parameters of these higher principles differed. The social contents and substances varied according to the socio-economic formations and orders in which the prophets lived.

This means that Islam is not a fixed idea or a rigid system of rituals, cults and institutions, but a progressive principle which always abrogates the old order of things. Musa abrogated the social order built by Ibrahim. 'Isa abrogated the economic order of Musa. Muhammad abrogated the social and economic institutions built by the preceding prophets. But all of them confirmed each other's truth. The truth was that all human beings are equal. They must be honest, speak the truth and struggle against the forces of evil, iniquity,oppression and falsehood. The institutions change, the customs vary but truth, equality and brotherhood remain as eternal principles of a free, just and equalitarian society.

17

TWO MORALITIES : REVOLUTIONARY AND FEUDALIST – CAPITALIST.

As we saw in details in the preceding pages, the prophet-revolutionaries, according to the Qur'an, were divinely inspired men of truth who fought against the forces of evil and falsehood and struggled to found communities of truth, social equality, love and brotherhood in different socio-economic formations and epochs. The truth in its essence and purpose was always the same: to destroy falsehood (*batil*) and oppression (*Zulm*) and to work for the emancipation of the oppressed.

The methods of emancipating the weak and oppressed, the socio-economic contents, subjects and systems, structures, superstructures and the modes of perceiving this social reality have always changed. The oppressors and good-kings who used brute force in the times of Nuh, Ibrahim or Musa to destroy the weak were not different from the hard-hearted and arrogant usurer-merchants and slave-owners of the Hijaz of the early seventh century A.D. in their falsehood, greed and oppression of the weak, but the social realities, economic conditions of their various societies were not the same. The god-kings of Chaldea and Egypt and the usurer-merchants of the Hijaz had one common trait: they opposed truth, human equality and brotherhood.

The fundamental aim of prophets' mission and revolution was to proclaim truth and establish a community of truth. This meant a total change in the old social structure which was divided into broad opposing social groups and classes of oppressors and oppressed, masters and slaves. The revolutionary process was a prolonged struggle between the forces of truth and falsehood, and in the case of early Islam, this struggle spread over a period of twenty three years.

In this revolutionary struggle new structures, new institutions, ideas, principles and rules emerged. In the new transformation, these revolutionary principles and rules took the place of old and dead principles. In the revolutionary struggle of early Muslims under the great prophet-revolutionary Muhammad, *Salat* and *Zakat* emerged as two very important social principles to weld the emergent Muslim-revolutionries into a well-knit community of truth and social equality. These two important concepts are here analysed to delineate the underlying tensions and contradictions between revolutionary and feudalist-capitalist moralities.

1. The Concepts of Salat and Zakat.

Literally *Salat* means supplication, entreaty, petition, prayer or communion with a higher moral or spiritual power. It is a constant remembrance and a perpetual supplication and submission of one's will to the higher Divine will. It is the conformity of one's whole self to the natural and Divine law which governs the universe.

Salat is the solicitation of truth and higher ideals of equality, love, brotherhood, selflessness on the part of those "who are endued with understanding (of truth) that receive admonition; those who fulfil the covenant of God (of conformity to truth) and fail not in their pledge;

those who join together those things which God hath commanded to be joined, hold their Lord in awe, and fear the terrible reckoning; those who patiently persevere seeking the countenance of their Lord; establish *Salat*; spend out of what We have bestowed for their sustenance, secretly and openly; and turn off evil with good: for such there is the final attainment of the (Eternal) Home." (13: 19–22).

Salat is thus the nexus, the communion and connection which binds everything, every living being, stars, the moon, the sun, birds and trees, animals and human beings to the Divine or the natural fountainhead and source of life, movement and struggle, energy and power both physical and moral: "Seest thou not that it is God whose praises all beings in the heavens and earth do celebrate, and the birds (of the air) with wings outspread? Each one knows its own (mode of) *salat* (prayer) and praise (*tasbiḥ*). And God knows well all that they do. Yea, to God belongs the dominion of the heavens and the earth; and to God is the final goal (of all)'" (24: 41–42).

Salat is the pivot on which every thing turns; it is the remembrance of the highest ideal, divine, natural or supranatural: it is the connection which connects every heart (and mind), to the highest source of energy or power. It means that in the social context the Quranic concept of *salat* underlines a sytem or behaviour of an ideal morality which is directly related to the values or principles of truth, social equality, justice, love of the poor and social responsibility.

Salat is the call for help and guidance to some transcendental power by a fighter in struggle against the forces of corruption, tyranny, injustice, ignorance, darkness and superstition. *Salat* is the heart of struggle, the essence and fruit of perseverance, patience and righteousness of an unceasing fighter against falsehood, *batil*. "O ye who believe", urges the Qur'an to the early Muslim revolutionaries who were struggling against oppressors and autocrats of all sorts and types," seek help with patient perseverance and *salat*, for God is with those who patiently persevere. And say not of those who are slain in the way of God: They are dead, they are living though ye perceive not. Be sure We will test you with something of fear and hunger, some loss in wealth or lives or the fruits but give glad tidings to those who patiently persevere, who say when afflicted with calamity: 'to God we belong and to Him is our return'. They are those on whom (descend) blessings from God and Mercy and they are the ones that receive Guidance." (2: 153–157).

It shows that *salat* is broader in conception than the narrow legalistic and mechanical mode of certain ritualistic genuflections and prostrations. It is not a mere verbal utterance of some esoteric formulae or 'magic' words the performance of which is considered to absolve people from their moral responsibilities to their fellow beings. Describing the lofty moral conduct of various peophet-revolutionaries the Qur'an says: "And We made them leaders guiding (mankind) by Our Command and We sent them inspiration to do good deeds, to establish *salat* and to practise *Zakat* and they constantly served us." (21: 73; 14: 37–41 and 19: 55).

In his strenuous efforts for establishing an equalitarian and just society the prophet-revolutionary is, for his own guidance and inspiration, always in direct and constant touch with the final fountainhead of all morality, goodness, knowledge, power and wisdom, the real force behind the ephemeral outward phenomena. He and his revolutionaries, share their wealth, food, raiment and every thing they possess with their companions so that their hearts are lifted and purified of all thoughts of greed, lust, selfishness, conceit and acquisitive impulses.

Zakat is not a charity, ritual or dole, it is rather a symbol of sacrifice, love and fellow-feeling for the oppressed. *Salat* and *Zakat* were not legal rituals but creative moral principles of an equalitarian and just society of early revolutionary Islam. (23: 1–11; and 2: 83). *Salat* and *Zakat* thus denoted the social and economic principles of a society based on truth and social equality. Without truth and social equality *salat* and *Zakat* become meaningless and lifeless rigid rituals, as empty shells without their essential cores.

Salat is a universal concept, a timeless awareness of the moral proposition, of social ideal of economic justice, love and brotherhood; it cannot be confined to any form, ritual, time, or place. It is a consciousness of the sublime, a means to achieve higher moral ends which make human beings free and noble, equal and precious: "So your God is One God: submit then your will to Him and give thou the good news to those who humble themselves. To those whose hearts, when God is mentioned, are filled with fear, who show patient perseverance over their afflictions, keep up *Salat,* and spend out of what We have bestowed upon them." (22: 34–35). *Salat* is the soul and spirit of the revoultionary who strives with his might and main for the cause of truth and equality, the cause for which he sacrifices everything, his possessions and even his life.

Prayer or *salat* is affirmed or justified only when man's whole conduct, thought, deeds, words and actions conform to truth, when he wholeheartedly dedicates his being to the cause of truth, the straight path, the path of truth, sincerity and integrity: "For Him (alone) is prayer in truth: any others they call upon besides Him hear them no more than if they were to stretch forth their hands for water to reach their mouth but it reaches them not; for the prayer of those without faith (in truth) is nothing but (futile) wandering in the mind." (13:14).

In this beautiful parable the Qur'an compares those who pray without conforming to a life of truth to a person who wants to drink with flatly stretched hands but cannot take water to his thirsty mouth. The hypocritical prayers of those who lead false lives of untruth are futile and senseless, without purpose and direction, without any goal or aim.

As a revolutionary principle *salat* was therefore a means or a mould which impressed and inculcated in the revolutionaries the moral courage to speak the truth, the boldness to face the oppressors, the patience to bear pains and adversities with calmness, and forbearance and strength to shun greed, lust and selfishness. *Salat* made them conscious of truth, social-equality, brotherhood and love of suffering humanity. *Salat* was thus a means and not an end. Those who take *salat* in the sense of a mere legal ritual performance of which absolves them of all moral responsibilities towards society (of speaking the truth etc.) are wrong and misled, like a person who gropes in the dark.

Any prayer cut off from the social and moral nexus is like a fruit without its core or a well without its water, or a dead body without its soul. This is the reason that the early mystics of Islam who had revolted against the overt legalism and hypocritical external performance of rituals taught by the Jurists (*Fuqaha*), had rightly taken *salat* as means (*Wasa'it*) to achieve higher values and moral realities, (*Haqa'iq*) of truth, purity of heart, innocence, identity of heart and mind, and of belief (thought) and action, love of the poor, equality, justice and selflessness.

Salat or prayer is in reality a ceaseless struggle of a revolutionary dedicated to the cause of truth and social equality; it is a constant war against the forces of evil and falsehood, injustice, and oppression. It is patience and perseverance, forbearance and resolute determination against the oppressors: "O my son" so advises Luqman, the wise man who was an African slave and a carpenter and who rejected wealth and high offices for the cause of truth, "establish *salat,* enjoin what is just and forbid what is wrong and bear with patient constancy whatever afflicts thee, for this perseverance is (a quality of those) who are resolute, determined and firm in their (noble) purpose". (31: 17). Prayer or *salat* is that state of mind and the condition of heart of a revolutionary who does not associate other gods with God who is the source of all power, goodness, knowledge and wisdom; which means that he only prays who is devoted to truth and who does not bow to human gods, selfish passions and lusts, false appearances, untruth, arrogance and injustice. He is a relentless fighter for social equality.

This is the conception of a revolutionary *salat.* But under feudalism when a counter-revolution destroyed the egalitarian society of Islam, the upper classes of lords and masters, kings and priests enslaved the broad masses. The concepts of Islamic revolution, like *Salat,* were used as political instruments to give a mere artificial semblance to a community divided into antagonistic classes, groups, dissensions and schisms. The jurists developed the legalistic and ritualistic conception of *salat* as a mere external performance of an act without having any concern for the purity of heart or for other virtues.

In early Islam, any act which aided the emancipation of the oppressed was a righteous deed; to speak the truth was a righteous deed; to establish a society on the basis of social equality was a righteous action; and to wage war against oppression was the real righteousness. But according to feudalist morality mere performance of *salat,* some formal genuflections and prostrations, were enough and entitled a person to become a 'faithful' even if he lied, fornicated and oppressed the slaves and the poor workers.

This seems to be a compromise of the ruling classes with the evil forces of feudalism which led to the destruction of all social morality of truth, social equality, justice, brotherhood and social solidarity. A class society is inherently inimical to the Quranic teachings. Feudalism distorted and disfigured the revolutionary concepts of pristine Islam.

2. The Concept of Zakat:

According to the Qur'an, *Zakat* (literally purification) was the fundamental principle of distributive justice under revolutionary Islam. It essentially aimed at removing the economic and social inequality, and sharing of all wealth of the community by all. "They ask you (O Prophet!) how much they should spend; say what is beyond your needs (*al-'afw*). Thus God makes clear to you His Signs in order that ye may meditate."(2: 219). "They ask you what they should spend: say whatever you spend of wealth is for parents and kindred and orphans, for the poor and the wayfarers. And whatever you spend of wealth, verily God knows it well." (2: 215).

As a principle the early Muslim revolutionaries owned means of production and sources of sustenance in common, because revolutionareis, whose aim is to destroy the old unequal social and economic structures, do not believe in private property. The prophet-revolutionary Muhammad did not leave private property, land, garden, slave, cattle, gold or silver after his dealth. Wealth, cattle, food and other consumer's goods surplus to the basic needs and requirements of a Muslim revolutionary were given to those who lacked them.

This was an act of righteousness since every act which mitigated the misery of the poor and aided in their emancipation from slavery and want was a righteous act. "Righteousness lies in giving wealth out of love of God (truth and social equality) for the kindred, for orphans and for the poor, for the wayfarers, for the destitute and for emancipating slaves (and righteous are those) who establish *salat* and pay *Zakat*. . ." (2: 177). "And *Sadaqat* are for the poor and the needy. . . ."(9:60).

Explaining the hypocrisy (*Nifaq*) of some beduins and residents of Medina, the Qur'an talks about a certain category of contemporary people "who confess their sins as they mix good deeds with bad deeds. God may return to them, verily God is Forgiving, Merciful. Take (O Prophet!) *Sadaqa* from their wealth so that it will clean and purify them (*tuzakkihim*). . . . . ."(9: 102–103).

3. Function of Zakat:

Thus the basic function of *Zakat* or *sadaqa* taken out of Muslims' wealth was two-fold: (1) to remove economic and social disparity and establish an egalitarian social order; (2) payment of a part of their wealth, ideally surplus over their basic needs, purified Muslims of their sins, imperfections, and bad deeds since parting with a major portion of their wealth was a sacrifice, an altruistic and righteous act. Economic inequality, which breeds evils in a community, is a social defect, deficiency and weakness whereas economic equality is strength and social solidarity.

This was the original revolutionary conception of *Zakat* and *Sadaqa* according to the Qur'an. As revolutionaries the early Muslims and the great Prophet shared their wealth with each other. As there was not enough to eat and wear in this pre-feudal society wealth surplus to the needs of a person was given as *sadaqa* and *Zakat* to those who had nothing to eat and wear. In early Islam, it appears, that *sadaqa* included consumer goods as well as fruit-trees, wells and orchards. This can be easily understood because Islam arose as a revolutionary social movement against social and economic inequality and against the concomitant moral and religious corruption of the Arab society of the early seventh century A.D.

By the Quranic concepts of *Salat* and *Zakat*, in general, are meant(1) the high moral values of truth, honesty, goodness, love, brotherhood and human equality, and(2) sharing of social or communal wealth and means of production in common, by all the members of the community without any distinction. These two concepts, ideas or systems of social morality and social economy were the two cornerstones of the social revolution brought by the prophet-revolutionaries.

The prophet Musa had also made these two principles the fundamental rules of the just community built by him. The Israelites had pledged under the shadow of the mount Sinai after their liberation from the slavery of the Egyptians that they would follow these high moral values of truth, equality and collective sharing of wealth, but they betrayed the trust. In the words of the Qur'an:

"God did aforetime take a covenant from the children of Israel and We appointed twelve captains among them and God said: 'I am with you, if ye(but) establish *salat* (the moral values of truth etc), practise *Zakat*, believe in My apostles, honour and assist them, and loan to God a beautiful loan, verily I will wipe out from you your evils, and admit you to Gardens with rivers flowing beneath; but if any of you, after this resisteth (truth), he hath truly wandered from the path of rectitude". (5: 12).

The Israelites rejected the Message of truth and social equality and in their false ways and rituals misinterpreted the words of the scripture, changing the meaning of the words out of their context or misapplying them on changed conditions, thus indulging in hypocrisy and double-dealing, "But because of their breach of their Covenant We cursed them and made their hearts grow hard. They change the words from their(right) places and forget a good part of the Message that was sent."(5: 13).

The same has happened with the Muslims who have also breached their Covenant of establishing a social order of truth and equality, goodness and justice. They use the words of revolutionary Islam, like *Salat, Zakat, Jihad, taqwa,* etc. out of their context, thus distorting the original meaning, essence, substance and purpose of the concepts. They interpret these concepts according to their own selfish desires, ulterior motives, and fancies.

4. Feudal Economic Morality:

In contradistinction to this egalitarian-revolutionary conception of *Zakat,* in the late decades of the first century of Hijra (early eighth century A.D.) when administrative and fiscal policies and practices had crystallized in the newly conquered lands, a feudalist concept of Zakat, that is, of fixed legalistic and ritualistic rate of tax, an officially prescribed levy of a feudal regime, emerged under new economic and social relationships when the Muslim community moved from a pre-feudal to a feudal formation.

'Umar ibn 'Abd al-'Aziz (i.e. 'Umar II), the pious Umayyad Caliph, says Malik ibn Anas (d. 179/795) in his *Muwatta,'* wrote to his governor at Damascus that *Sadaqa* or Zakat-tax was to be collected on agricultural produce, precious metals and cattle only. And Malik says that his legal opinion is that *sadaqa* can only be levied on these three types of goods. This legal principle of *Zakat*, according to Malik, is based on a legal tradition of the Prophet which has been related on the authority of the famous companion of the prophet: Abu Sa'id al-Khudri (d. 74/693). Malik relates from 'Amr ibn Yahya al-Mazini, who relates from his father that he heard Abu Sa'id al-Khudri saying: "The Apostle of God said that there was no *sadaqa* on less than five camels, five *awqiyas* of silver (i.e. forty dirhams), five *awsaq* (i.e. sixty measures of *sa's*) wheat, barley, dates etc. That is, five camels, forty dirhams and sixty *sa's* of food-grains were taxable for *Zakat*.

If this tradition is genuine it reflectes the economic conditions of a subsistence economy of scarcity. Abu Sa'id al-Khudri died in the year 74 when under the early Umayyads specific social, economic and legal relationships of a feudalist hierarchy consolidated. The revolutionary concepts of pristine Islam were politically used to legitimize the regime. Under the circumstance, *Zakat* now becomes a mere ritualistically prescribed legal tax analogous to the prescribed ritual of *Salat*. *Zakat* becomes a feudalist category: a levy imposed by an autocratic feudal regime without its egalitarian substance, and its purpose of emancipating the oppressed classes and for establishing an egalitarian social order. The purpose is now to enslave the oppressed classes of slaves, serfs and workers.

The revolutionary concept of *Zakat* was a principle for levelling down disparity between the rich and the poor, for emancipating slaves from the bondage of oppressors, but the feudal principle of *Zakat* was reduced to a prescribed minimal and nominal rate to rationalize the Umayyad *Fisk* and the feudal economic relationships, slavery, serfdom and exploitation of the lower classes.

There were thus two concepts of *Zakat* or two kinds of economic morality. First, *Zakat* as a revolutionary principle of social and economic equality, and secondly, *Zakat* as a feudalist principle of maintaining inequalities and disparities, thus becoming a principle of charity, a mere ritual in the hands of the rich, a sanctimonious instrument to calm the qualms of a guilty conscience. This shows that the minimal rate of *Zakat* discussed by the Jurists is a feudal category which is a mere ritual without the real and original moral substance which was to remove social and economic inequality in a radical way.

Under the modern system of capitalism industrial and finance capital has predominated all production processes. Modern means of production, factories and machines, raw-materials and inventories, economic institutions of joint stock companies, credit and banking institutions have all developed during the last four centureies (17th–20th). The literal application of *Zakat* on agricultural produce, precious metals (or money), and cattle would then exclude all modern industrial capital from *Zakat* which clearly means that big capitalists will be exempted from the levy of *Zakat* under 'Islamic' capitalism and all burden will be on the lower middle classes and the workers.

This means that the concepts and ideas of revolutionary Islam have been misinterpreted and misapplied in a modern economy and society to suit the interests of the rich upper classes. And that the political economy of *Zakat* in the mixed capitalist economy of Pakistan is an anachronism and scientifically speaking, a reactionary and retrogressive policy which has nothing to do with the original Quranic concept of *Zakat*.

The two examples of *Salat* and *Zakat* therefore prove that the two moralities, revolutionary and feudalist-capitalist, are opposed to each other. The former aimed at producing men of truth, honesty, integrity and sincerity who struggled for social equality and brotherhood. On the other hand, the latter manipulated the principles and rules of early Islam out of their real context in order to subjugate the broad masses. The concepts of early Islam, like *Salat*, Zakat, *sadaqa* etc., operated in a pre-feudal social formation. The social reality conformed to these concepts and ideas. But under feudalism and capitalism, as social conditions changed, the early concepts were used to preserve the exploitative systems.

The feudalist-capitatist morality created a dangerous gap betweeen legalistic ritual and morality. Prescription of a legal ritual, official prayer at fixed times and places, and an official fixed rate of *Zakat* became rituals and cults, external and ostentatious performance of which came to be considered acts of piety even if the performer was a liar and murderer in his personal life. This too much stress on an outward legal and prescribed act cut the very roots of social morality; it bypassed the inner conscience and purity of heart and mind. It obliterated all distinctions between truth and falsehood, honesty and dishonesty, right and wrong, justice and injustice.

In this attitude of mind one pretends something which he does not possess. One becomes a hypocrite and ostensibly does an act which he does not believe in his heart. This makes religion a cover or facade for lies, falsehood, oppression and exploitation. Hypocritical behaviour, mere lipservice to the pristine principles of the revolutionary Islam divest all moral essence from social conduct and removes the real meaning from concepts and ideas. The revolutionary principles of *Salat, Zakat, Jihad,* (war) *Hijra* (migration) etc. were directly related to the establishment of a social order of truth, social equality and brotherhood.

Jihad and *Hijra* were the righteous acts of dedicated revolutionaries who fought against the oppressors and tyrants and left their hearths and homes, lands and wealth for the cause of truth. But under feudalism and capitalism all these principles of pristine Islam have been turned into citadels of vested interests, into political instruments to suppress the poor and exploit them.

This gap between the legalistic ritual and morality has destroyed the social, economic, political and intellectual processes in our society because, when the moral fibre is sapped social vitality and strength are corroded from inside. The social core begins to rot as there is no moral foundation or basic rules or principles on which the social edifice could arise. This gap can only be bridged by a radical change and revolution which could restructure the entire social, economic and moral order on new foundations, new principles and a new *Weltanschauung* replacing the present decadent systems of capitalism and feudalism in Pakistan and in other third world countries.

In the present social and economic conditions of a retarded and dependent capitalism in the Muslim societies, the Imperialists are using religion to arrest all progress and popular movement towards a radical social change. They are resurrecting Sufism or mysticism to channelize social energy, and impending revolt of the oppressed masses, toward mystic interiorization, or entangling them in their (meta) psychological aberrations.

Sufism cannot bring any social revolution, because in its origins, it was a passive reaction of rebels against feudal oppression.

As we have explained in the preceding pages, the original Islamic social movement was a revolt of the oppressed against the forces of evil, inequality, injustice and exploitation. The early Muslim revolutionaries stood for the principles of truth and social equality. But when under the Umayyad autocrats feudalism reasserted itself in the forms of social divisions and new socio-economic relations of masters and slaves, lords and serfs, the entire ideological (super) structures, of new beliefs and concepts, was formulated by the jurists to rationalize the feudal relations. The concept of a legalistic Sharia or religio-social law was developed which tended to rigidify the early concepts into ossified legalistic rituals without their inner essence of equality and brotherhood.

The early mystics revolted against this lifeless legalism of the concept of *Sharia* which had bypassed inner values of truth, sincerity, selflessness, love, brotherhood, equality etc. and gave undue emphasis to mere outward performance of rituals. This ritualism killed all social morality and bred hypocrisy, outward religiosity, simulation, false and superficial external behaviour.

This shows that political use of religion by the Imperialists whether in the form of crass fundamentalism, for social suppression of masses' revolt against feudalism and capitalism, or for propagating the archaic types of *Sufism*, is primarily aimed at obstructing the path of radical social change and revolution in the third-world societies. Only a modern social revolution guided by modern science and rational attitude of mind, can emancipate the oppressed working classes. Religious attitude and perception cannot solve the social problem in modern societies.

18

PROPHETS AND REVOLUTIONARIES

1. Prophecy and Liberation Theology:

The prophet-revolutionaries, according to the Qur'an, were divinely inspired leaders of the oppressed classes of their respective communities. They were helped and guided by the divine, moral, natural, and historical forces on the right path of truth, human equality and brotherhood. Prophets were the custodians and trustees of truth. They had Covenant (*Mithaq*) with God, that they would faithfully carry out their mission, proclaim God's truth which they had discovered.

The aim of prophecy was to eliminate *Zulm* (oppression, inequality) from the face of th earth, and to guide and enlighten humanity on the right path. "And remember," says the Quran, We took from the prophets their Covenant as (We did) from thee (O Muhammad!): from Nuh, Ibrahim, Musa and 'Isa, the son of Maryam. We took from them a solemn Covenant that (God) may question the (custodians) of truth concerning the Truth they (were charged with). And He has prepared for the rejecters (of truth) a grievous penalty." (33: 7–8).

The prophet-revolutionaries were thus righteous human beings and on the right path. "These were the men to whom We gave the Book and authority and Prophethood. . ." (6: 83–89). Prophecy is the means, the agency, the method to liberate the oppressed and guide them on the path of truth. Its fountainhead and source is the divine power, goodness, mercy, knowledge and wisdom.

But we live under revolutionary times. Modern age is the era of science and reason. Great transformations in society and in thought are taking place rapidly. The modern world stands divided into two polarized social and economic systems of capitalism and socialism. This polarization and contrast have also penetrated to the societies of the third-world in Asia, Africa and Latin America where class struggle between the powerful upper classes (the Bourgeoisie) and the oppressed lower classes (the Proletariat) are developing, sometimes latent and open, and sometimes armed and violent. The old socio-economic formations of feudalism under inevitable laws have changed and are changing into higher formations of capitalism and socialism. The revolutionary parties are waging class wars against the forces of capitalism and many countries have liberated themselves from the bondage of the capitalists, both local and foreign.

Amidst revolutionary class struggles in the third-world societies a typical ideology of liberation theology has been formulated in modern political terms although religious ideology has ceased to exist as a political force in the advanced western societies, both capitalist and socialist, where scientific culture, secular polity and rational behaviour have become standard social norms.

However, in the less developed societies of the third-world where pre-capitalist social formations co-exist with capitalist formations, such as in the Middle East countries, the religious scholars (*'ulama'*) have spearheaded a social revolution and have invoked religion and thelogy for refurbishing the panoply of class struggle against the forces of Imperialism. In Iran, after the revolution against the Shah and his oppressive regime, religious scholars have been endeavouring to develop a religious, political and social theory for reorganizing the old feudal-capitalist social order. Their theory of the 'rule of the jurisconsult' (*Wilayat al-faqih*) although feudalist in conception, is squarely based on the notion of liberation theology.

This concept of liberation theology assumes that the Qur'an and the teachings/sayings of the prophet Muhammad fundamentally aimed at establishing a society in which the *Fuqaha,* the jurisconsults, played a pre-dominant role in decreeing prescriptions of definite social and economic conduct and policies. This concept further presumes that the Muslim *'Ulama'* have the right to rule in a Muslim society because they are custodians and trustees of the Prophet's legacy of knowledge and wisdom—*'Ulama'* are the heirs of the prophets'. But *Fiqh,* or the medieval Muslim law gradually developed in the feudal era, that is, in the post-Quranic times. The entire *Fiqh* literature is the product of feudalism. It cannot be equated to the revolutionary Islam of the Qur'an. The feudal Islam rationalized the feudal institutions and thus legitimized the stratification of Muslim society into freemen and slaves, lords and serfs, oppressors and oppressed, kings and their suppressed subjects. This social hierarchy was clearly contrary to the egalitarian teachings of the Qur'an.

In Lebanon, Libya, Syria, South Yemen and elsewhere some political elements have also been using religion in their ideological fight against Imperialism and capitalist-feudalist classes. They think that Islam was a revolutionary movement in its beginning. Islam emancipated the weak social classes in the past, and it can again deliver the goods and emancipate the modern proletariat from the slavery of the ruling bourgeoisie.

Similarly there is a tendency in the Latin American counties, among the ecclesiastics, to supplement the revolutionary class struggle with the egalitarian teachings and traditions of early Christianity. According to them, in its origins, Christianity was actually a social movement of the downtrodden and poor workers against the rampant social inequality, religious degeneration and moral decay of the Roman society in the Near East. They maintain that Jesus Christ was himself a worker and his disciples were washermen, carpenters, weavers and workers of humble and lowly origins.

Both these religious groups, Islamic and Christian, fundamentalist or liberal-progressive, use medieval religion and theology for the cherished aim of emancipating the subjugated masses and working classes from the oppression of the capitalists, thus linking the modern class struggle of capitalist societies to the prophets' missions in the feudal and pre-feudal ancient societies.

In this chapter we shall discuss the nature of this ideology of liberation theology with special reference to the Islamic religion and theology.

We shall examine the probable hypothesis as to whether this ideology can be interpreted as a reflection of the contemporary pastoral-tribal and (semi)– feudal social structures of the many third-world countries, Muslim lands in particular, which have strong imprints of the fixed religious frameworks and modes of perception, and where no industrial, social and scientific revolutions have taken place, nor has any movement of reformation reformulated religion and religious conceptions of life, nature and history, as it happened in Europe where social and industrial revolutions of the seventeenth and eighteenth centuries liberated man and his mind from feudal restraints.

According to the Qur'an, the prophet-revolutionries, Ibrahim, Musa, 'Isa and Muhammad were the divinely inspired leaders of the weak and exploited lower social classes. These prophets, humble, courageous, honest and self-effacing in appearance and moral conduct stood for truth, enlightenment, human equality, brotherhood, love and goodness. As they were divinely inspired they were on the right path,*Sirat Mustaqim*; and after liberating the humble and downtrodden from iniquitous social orders (*Qura Zalima*) they tried to establish new orders of social justice, equality, true morality, a new *Weltanschauung,* a paradise on earth. (14: 1–4).

On the opposite side stood pharaohs, the god-kings, the corrupt and insolent rulers who exercised absolute power and brute force to stifle truth, justice, equality and goodness. They were embodiments of greed, falsehood, pride, ignorance, iniquity and superstition–the forces of evil and darkness. They were astray from the right path.

Prophets and pharaohs, men of God and men of Evil were, thus, two anti-thetical and contraditory forces, two opposite orders, or systems of goodness and evil, truth and falsehood, light and darkness, knowledge and ignorance, faith and superstition. The men of God or prophet-revolutionaries represented the oppressed and exploited–the people thrown into the dust. The men of Evil or pharaohs led the powerful and rich upper classes.

This struggle between the masters and their slaves, the powerful and the weak, took place in the pre-feudal times when methods of perceiving reality and modes of interpreting the social, natural and historical phenomena were mainly religious and supernatural and were fixed in their basic thought patterns. The social formations in which the prophets and pharaohs, kings and lords, masters and high priests and the lowly masses lived and moved, thought and reflected were pastoral-tribal and pre-feudal.

This shows that before they were institutionalized and ossified into lifeless rituals, cults, customs, preserved by vested interestes, these social movements led by divinely inspired prophet-revolutionaries, like Ibrahim, Musa and Muhammad, primarily aimed at liberating the oppressed lower classes (termed by the Qur'an as *al-mustad'afun* and *al-ardhalun).* Thus theology and eschatology, as in the Qur'an, essentially underline, first, liberation and salvation of the exploited, and secondly, destruction of he iniquitous social orders based on untruth, oppression and superstition.

In its simple, down to earth parables, similes, metaphors and allegories from nature and history, the Qur'an compares prophets and pharaohs to two extremes: Divine and Satanic. (Remember also) the 'Ad and Thamud (people)," says the Qur'an, "clearly will appear to you

> from (the traces) of their buildings (their fate): the Evil one made their deeds alluring to them, and kept them back from the (right) path, though they were gifted with intelligence and skill. (Remember also) Qarun, Pharaoh, and Haman: there came to them Moses with Clear Signs, but they behaved with insolence on the earth ; yet they could not overreach(Us). Each one of them We seized for his crime: of them against some We sent a violent tornado (with showers of stone); some were caught by a (mighty) Blast; some We caused the earth to swallow up; and some We drowned (in the waters). It was not God Who injured (or oppressed) them. They injured (and oppressed) their own souls. The parable of those who take protectors other

than God is that of the spider who builds (to itself) a house; but truly the flimsiest of houses is the spider's house: if they but knew." (29: 38–41).

Intoxicated with power and puffed up with wealth and pride the Pharaoh had enslaved the people of *Israel*. "Indeed Pharaoh elated himself in the land and broke up its people into groups and classes, depressing a class of people among them: their sons he slew, but he kept alive their females; for he was indeed a perpetuator of corruption." (28: 4).

Musa (Moses) liberated his people from the slavery of the Egyptian Pharaoh many centureis before the birth of Jesus Christ. The prophets' social mission was thus to liberate the suffering masses from economic, social, spiritual and moral bondage and then establish a just and equalitarian order. This is the basic idea of liberation theology in the pre-capitalist social formations, simplified in the fixed religious idiom and allegorical language and expression of the times. Prophecy, divine inspiration, ravelation of truth as a whole, contradictions between truth and falsehood, belief and disbelief of divine message, forces of goodness and evil were the principal categories of this religious ideology of liberation.

2. Problem of Perception.

Every age and society perceives the reality of its existence and environment in a specific social and economic formation and in a given situation in which the society moves. The society explains and understands the natural and social phenomena with the mental capacities, intellectual capabilities and skills, methods and apparatuses at its disposal.

The basic idea of liberation theology as a divinely

inspired mission and a revelatory truth, although social in content, was inextricably intertwined with and fixed supernatural, or metaphysical framework because perception of reality and life, nature and history in the feudal and pre-feudal eras was thoroughly religious. That is, all thought, reflection, speculation, intellection, feeling, emotion and morality were refracted through the prism of religion. These were the ages of religion and 'faith'. Religion was the great simplifier of reality.

The Qur'an was revealed in the Hijaz during a period of twenty three years, about A.D. 610 to 632, to the prophet –revolutionary Muhammad ibn 'Abd Allah in a milieu where religion was the sole mode and medium of expression.

The one hundred and fourteen *Suras* or chapters of the Qur'an depict the struggle of the prophet-revolutionaries (from Adam to Muhammad) against the forces of evil and oppression as an eternal conflict between goodness and evil, right and wrong, light and darkness, in simple allegories and metaphors in order to explain human problems in simplified categories and enable the mind of the contemporary man to comprehend the message and act upon it. It is an invitation to think and reflect and then to act upon it. The discovery of truth, knowledge and wisdom was made accessible to the ordinary and humble human beings, the oppressed and exploited, weak and lowly, without the intercession of scholars and high priests. Truth is always simple and direct.

Truth was perceived and explained in a simplified way God, Divine Power, Energy or Force behind natural, social, human and historical phenomena was conceived by man of religious mentality, as anthropomorphic. God was conceived as source of all power, force, energy, knowledge, wisdom, creation, evolution, mercy, and judgement. 'He has power over every thing', 'Every thing belongs to Him' 'Every thing will return to Him,' 'He has dominion over the entire Universe', are the oft-repeated verses of the holy Qur'an. With the prophet-revolutionary whose heart and mind are the receptacles of revelatory truth, enlightement and guidance, divine presence is a highly intense sense of responsibility, consciousness of truth and duty, accountability and sympathy. He suffers with the suffering massess.

He undergoes the agony of a Day of Judgement, within his own heart and mind; for him every moment is a trial, a judgement, a standing before the High Tribunal. Every moment he dies and lives. In the presence of God he becomes fearless, he neither frets nor grieves. He is resurrected from a material existence. He attains freedom and then he resurrects and emancipates the oppressed and suppressed human beings.

In this world of religious categories and allegorical simplifications the supranatural hierarchies of power and control of human destiny, more or less, reflected the social hierarchies of primitive, pastoral-tribal and (pre-) feudal societies, on the one hand, and precarious states of disorder, anarchy, chaos, fear and insecurity inherent in the social order, on the other. The common man, unlike the prophet-revolutionary, could not rise above his material existence and mode of perception and expression.

In his religious speculation, explanation and simplification man tries to understand, explain, conceive and relate what happens within him and around him, in allegorical terms. "And such are the parables (*amthal*) We set for mankind but only those understand them who have knowledge. God created the heavens and the earth in true (proportions): verily in that is a Sign (*ayat*) for those who believe". (29: 43–44).

3. Many Interpretations:

In a (pre-) feudal society, where natural and social sciences have not developed with their elaborate scientific methodology, a man will tend to interpret a certain event (social, natural or historical), rain, flood, war, earthquake, growth of crops, birth or death of an animal or an abnormal human behaviour, as something caused by one Highest Cause, directed by some Mysterious Power or Force. But after the development of natural, social and biological sciences and their scientific methodology in the modern era interpretation of these events has become sophisticated and scientific as many explanations or many causes–natural, social, geographical, economic, biological, psychological, etc,–are forthcoming to understand such phenomena in a correct way. Life, society and nature are a complex and many–faceted reality which, according to modern science, cannot be understood with simplifications of one cause only.

The very conception of God, supranatural Power or Force has evolved throughout the ages as human mind evolved. The truth discovered by the prophet-revolutionaries was in essence the same, but methods and forms for discovering the truth differed.

In a world ruled by brute force and crass selfishness, greed and lust, darkness and superstition every arrogant tyrant, king, priest, lord or tribal chief considered himself a god-king (*ilah*), and every related cult, ritual, idol, custom corrupt institution, depraved order, law, command and practice was, under coerceon and force to be taken as a standard, criterion, norm and model. Life tended to be a jungle where beasts preyed upon the weak and innocent, and the powerful devoured the helpless. This rule of jungle, social disorder and moral anarchy misled the ignorant common people.

In his religious coception man thus simplified the complex reality through simple categories of contradictions. Religion attributed goodness, harmony, wisdom and order in the cosmos to God: and evil, oppression, corruption, disorder, discord and superstition to Satan. The concept of Divine unity as a source of harmony, unity, morality, truth, equality and righteousness was preached by the prophets sent by God to this sin-stained world.

In this religious conception, unlike an earthly king or lord, God is the Lord and Nourisher of mankind, Creator of the unvierse and Sustainer of nature. He creates man, sustains him, cares for him, loves him; He rewards him for good deeds, and punishes him for sins and crimes. He is Just, full of mercy, knowledge and wisdom. "There is no god but He,–the Living, the Self-subsisting, Eternal. No slumber can seize Him nor sleep. His are all things in the heavens and on earth. Who is there can intercede in His presence except as He permitteth. He knoweth what (appears to His creatures as) before or after or behind them. Nor shall they compass aught of His knowledge except as He willeth. His throne doth extend over the Heavens and the earth, and He feeleth no fatigue in guarding and preserving them for He is the Most High, the Supreme (in glory)". (2: 255).

God sits on a lofty throne and manages human affairs according to His universal Plan. He does whatever He wants. There is no space and time in His Domain. Only God can guide man's conduct through darkness and lead him to bliss and salvation. The prophet-revolutionaries, as humble, tender-hearted, self-effacing men of truth submit their whole selves to the Will and Plan of God and to His ordained system of morality and social conduct.

To God will all return and account for their deeds

after the Great Resurrection, when sins committed during the probationary life of this world will be accounted for. The prophets and their followers seek help and guidance from Him against evil and must trust Him in their struggle against god-kings, tyrants and oppressors of weak human beings. For the tyrants the sources of power are wealth, brute force, armies, possessions and earthly domains, but for the prophets God is the source of all power, goodness, knowledge and wisdom.

This is the religious/theological conception of the mission of the prophets, their revelation and Divine guidance in the struggle of the weak people against the powerful pharaohs in he pre-capitalist social context.

4. God and Man:

In the anthropomorphic conception of God, a prophet is a divinely inspired human being and has direct communion with his God who guides him in this turbulent world. God helps him in his struggle against evil. 'God is nearer to man than his jugular vein.' His nearness and fervent awareness of God is the real source of morality, knowledge and wisdom and a standard of judgement between right and wrong, true and false. And fear of God is the beginning of wisdom. The prophet-revolutionary lives in the Presence of God. God guides him at every moment of his life.

Accordingly, death of a prophet is the end of his direct communion with God. The prophet of revolutionary Islam died in A.H.10/632 A.D. and there ceased the divine revelation to him. And his direct communion with his God came to an end. When the Muslim community territorially extended and moved to the feudal socio-economic formation the revolutionary 'elan of the pristine Islam was sapped.

In His transcendence God was interpreted by the Jurists and Traditionists to have given a closed system of morality once and for all, and then He removed Himself away from this sin-filled world, thus leaving a chasm, gap or space between God and man, since the prophet-revolutionary was no more there and the revolutionary principles came to be institutionalized as rigid and fixed cults and rituals bereft of their revolutionary essence and purpose.

The interspace between God and man, once filled with the divinely inspired prophet, was now tended to be filled by so many intercessors, intermediaries, priests, ecclesiastics, idols, groups of various forms of religio-political hues claiming divine powers and rights, half-men and half-gods. Innumerable institutions of vested interests crop up in this vacant space to exploit the religious sentiments of the poor and credulous masses. Grotesque notions and superstitions about the personality of the Prophets are fabricated to impress the ignorant masses that the Prophet is still alive in a spiritual form. Some religious elements make the Prophet a demi-God.

The religious interspace between God and man, exaggerated by the vested interests is exploited by the Imperialists and native capitalists, feudal lords and bureaucrats, both at intellectual and socio-political planes in the developing societies which still exist in feudal formations. Dubious religious ideologies are being devised, and pristine concepts and ideas of revolutionary missions of the prophets are being erroneously used to dull the minds of the common people and thus misguide them. Propagation of a traditionally rigidified religion with its feudalist/medievalist contents is aimed at crippling the creative and critical faculties of the people.

Emancipation of the weak by the divinely inspired prophets was the basic idea of liberation theology in the pre-capitalist times. But now under Imperialism, the traditional religion, in its institutionalized rigid form, is politically manipulated to keep masses in bondage and thraldom, using external religiosity, its cults and rituals to dull sense perception and to paralyse the mental, intellectual, moral and emotional feculties of the common people. Instead of radically changing the decaying social structures, relgion is used by the rulers in league with the Imperialists to perpetuate the corrupt feudal and capitalist institutions and to enslave the masses which ultimately destroys their critical and rational faculties, emotional vigour and moral courage.

Religion is often a decayed form of its pristine social movement and has, thus, lost its essential spiritual and social content and its original moral ethos. When the words of revealed scripture lose their meaning and spirit during the decaying process, they cannot be applied to changed social reality. Now the crucial question is this: Is this precapitalist ideology of liberation theology relevant to a modern revolutionay class-struggle which is a scientific process and not a religious proposition?

As we have seen in detail, the idea of liberation thelogy of emancipation of the weak by a divinely inspired prophet-revolutionary and the contradictory categories of prophets and pharaohs, goodness and evil, revelation and superstition were the products of a specific era of faith when, as the Qur'an explains, religion was the fixed framework and idiom for perceiving and expressing reality.

The prophets were divinely guided and had direct communion with God. Their conduct and teachings were the criterion for distinguishing right from wrong. However, with the development of modern sciences and intellectual capabilities of man in the modern era, perception of reality has changed from emotional-religious to rational-scientific. The scientific, democratic-popular, industrial and intellectual processes have not penetrated deeply into the precapitalist societies like Pakistan.

Unlike Europe of the sixteenth century A.D. when the traditional religion was reformed and transformed as a category subject to science and social philosophy, no radical religious reformation took place in the modern Muslim society. This is the reason that the ruling capitalists, landlords, bureaucrats, militarymen and high priests manipulate people's emotional attachment to religion by 'playing God' and advancing tendentious interpretations of the Qur'an and sayings of the Prophet to suit the social and economic ideology of capitalism. The masses are too simple to differentiate between a prophet's real and revolutionary social mission of social equality and subtleties of the ossified cults and rituals of a decayed religion; that is, between true and false. The masses find themselves in the marsh of a cultic, hypocritical and legalistic religion which has nothing to do with the original teachings of the peophet. The legalistic religion is rather a reversal of the revolutionary ideals of the Prophet. Here lie the dangers in the path of liberation theology.

As the term implies, theology was a liberator; the divinely inspired and guided prophet-revolutionary emancipated the slaves and serfs; but in the modern times, in the hands of the Imperialists and capitalists (modern pharaohs? to use the term of liberation theology) religion (and theology) has become an enslaving instrument. No prophets will come but 'pharaohs' have every where organized themselves into a formidable 'evil' force to oppress and enslave the poor masses, the proletariat who depend for their very existence on the means of production owned by the bourgeoisie. And the entire legacy of cultic religion, religious classes, ecclesiastics, their seminaries and feudalistic religious ideology stand on the side of the exploiters.

The political exploitation of religion by the ruling Imperialists and their paid ideologues removes ground from beneath the ideology of liberation theology because religion is used primarily to maintain a decadent *status quo*. Divested of inner morality and socio-economic substance, a cultic and ritualistic religion is an assortment of superstition, self-conceits, bigotry and obscurantism.

Moreover the objective conditions when a divinely inspired prophet could lead the suffering masses to salvation and when theology was a liberator, are not present in the modern society. Modern society is a class society and modern class-struggle is a scientific process. Now social revolutions transform decadent social systems into new social orders under certain scientific laws when one mode of production, as feudalism, yields its place to a higher mode of production, as capitalism. Such changes occur inevitably when certain conditions are fulfilled. Semi-feudal and capilalist societies, like those of Pakistan and other third-world countries, shall undergo similar social transformations, through evolution or revolution depending on the nature of class struggle which is some times latent and some times open, violent and radical.

Under modern conditions when the religious mode of perceiving and understanding reality has been replaced by scientific and rational methods and approaches, the concept of liberation theology, being a supernatural category of thought, then becomes irrelevant to modern class struggle. Liberation theology was a product of the pre-capitalist social conditions when oppressed classes used to be emancipated by a divinely inspired prophet through his direct communion with his God and revelations.

This was the fixed religious framework with its fixed categories of thought, perception and cognition. The discovery of truth by a prophet and his struggle against pharaohs and god-kings were all circumscribed by a religious-theological setting or mould in which were cast and impressed the ideas, emotions, concepts and practices of the times.

Modern society is a class society of capitalists and proletariat and between them lie numerous sub-classes of big capitalists, small capitalists and medium-sized capitalists and the classes subservient to them. The capitalists, in general, own major means of production: lands, mines, factories, and all capital resources. The proletariat lacks capital resources and sells its labour power to the capitalists in order to live.

All political power, legislative assemblies, administrative apparatuses, laws, religious institutions, and media are controlled and used by the ruling capitalists to suppress and exploit the working masses. Bourgeois democracy is a facade to cover this hegemony of the bourgeoisie.

This discussion then shows that only a scientifically organized revolutionary struggle and not liberation theology of ancient times, can liberate the modern working classes. The original conception of liberation theology as a revolutionary movement can assist as an auxhiliary aid to the larger class-struggle. But this use has its limits within the scientific method and modern revolution. This would then explain why the Iranian revolution which was initiated against the Imperialists has bogged down in the marshes of feudal 'Islam' and feudal socio-economic institutions which are erroneously taken as Islamic and revolutionary.

19

CONCLUSION.

The main purpose of this study was to investigate, in modesty and humility, the nature of the missions, movements, lives, roles and characters of the prophets as illustrated in the candid and cogent verses of the Qur'an. These prophets were divinely inspired and guided men of truth who appeared in different communities throughout the ages, in the pre-capitalist times.

As we saw in details in the consistent struggles of these prophets against the combined forces of evil, oppression and superstition, the ends of the prophet-revolutionaries were: proclamation of truth, emancipation of the poor proletariat and lastly, establishment of social equality.

The prophets lived, worked and struggled in the pre-capitalist and pre-industrial social formations when social reality was seen, perceived and expressed through the language and idiom of religion. Religion as a method of perception and expression of reality was a great simplifier of social and natural phenomena and their mysteries and laws. Religion employed imagery and allegory of parables, similes and examples to illustrate problems of nature, society and history. Divine inspiration and revelation of truth to a man of God was explained to the contemporary world in down-to-earth illustrations from nature, rivers, plants, rain, clouds, mountains, animals and humble insects like bees, mosquitoes, ants, spiders etc. Religion was thus a primitive science and truth was reflected and expressed through the prism of religion.

Revolutions or social changes brought by the prophet -revolutionaries occurred in this religious framework: the categories of thought, patterns of behaviour, sensibilities, emotions and morals were all impressed and conditioned in the religious mould and mentality.

Modern science is an improvement over religious mentality in the sense that science as method of observation, experimentation, and perception of social reality originated when natural, social and biological sciences began to be separated from theology and human mind was liberated from the strictures of religion when industrial, social and religious transformations took place in the 16th-18th centuries. Scientific mehod gradually evolved to replace religious perception and approach.

Religion traced all chances and changes in society, nature and history to the single Divine cause, but science tries to relate changes and movements in the phenomena to various, mysterious causes which are discoverable by human mind. This liberation of mind and human thought gave impetus to the development of modern sciences—natural, biological and social. For science truth is not final but tentative as was originally the conception of Godhead discovered by the prophets of yore.

Similarly modern class struggle, the antagonism between capitalist and working classes cannot be understood without the help of modern science. Modern social revolution is a scientific process and modern revolutionaries are scientists and not prophets because modern method of seeing and perceiving social reality, social change and social revolution is no more religious and theological relating everything to One Cause. Human knowledge has exploded, truth has ramified and society has become a complex organism, and without modern science the phenomena cannot be understood and explained correctly. And without correct understanding no society can be changed and no revolution can fructify.

According to the Qur'an, God sends rain and revives dead societies, destroys corrupt social orders and reveals truth to His chosen men of truth and purity. These are religious statements, simple, pithy, frank, full of mystery, wonder and beauty relating everything to God who is the only source of life, power, mercy, knowledge and wosdom. Between God, human mind and the natural social phenomena there is a vast space, potentiality, mystery to be known, explored and investigated by the human mind. Man was destined to find out in a scientific way the cause of cloud formations which bring rain, the social processes according to which societies rise, decay and fall. Through science and reason man could discover the laws which governed the rise and fall of human civilizations. Man developed social and natural sciences to discover the mysteries left unexplored by the religious method of the medieval ages. Science is an improvement upon religion as a method of perceiving and changing social reality.

It is then not difficult to understand that the religious and theological revelations of truth to the prophet-revolutionaries are related to pre-industrial societies. This divinely revealed truth, as stated earlier, aimed at emancipating the suffering humanity from evil and oppression. The mission of the prophets' movements and struggles was to establish a society based on the principles of truth and social equality.

The aim of modern social revolutions is also to set up a social order of equality, brotherhood and love where no capitalists and landlords can oppress and exploit the working classes. But methods of liberation have changed. Liberation theology has been replaced by (liberation) science.

Why does religious mentality still persist in the underdeveloped societies of the third world, like Pakistan? And why is religion exploited by the ruling classes of capitalists, landlords and bureaucrats for political purposes? This is because pre-capitalist socio-economic formations still co-exist with the capitalist structures in Pakistan. These feudal and pastoral-tribal social structures are peculiarly characteristic of religious mentality as science, industry and technology have not penetrated deeply into them. This is the reason that the poor and illiterate masses strongly cling to religion and tradition.

The ruling classes who monopolize all national wealth, education, political power, privileges, also exploit this fact and control religion, its cults and rituals for conserving and consolidating their hold on the economy and society. They are in league with the foreign capitalists who use religion as a political instrument to control and suppress the working classes and masses. The divinely-inspired prophets used religion and theology to liberate the oppressed people but the modern capitalists use this ossified religion to enslave, confuse and paralyse the working classes.

Exploitation of religion is a highly dangerous act which destroys the social and moral fabric of the entire society. When prophets do not come and prophecy has ceased to link man with God, religion must yield its place to science so that human problems are understood and solved in a correct way, otherwise the space between God and man will be filled up by numerous demi-gods, pseudo-prophets, *pirs,* false teachers, preachers, impostors and charlatans who will mislead the simple masses and collaborate with the ruling classes to oppress the poor and the downtrodden.

This is the age of science, reason and revolution. The societies which still use religion to perceive, understand and change the natural and social phenomena are doomed to extinction. Religion, in the form of ossified and rigid rituals is dead; it cannot solve human problems. Only modern scientific method can help man observe, experiment and perceive the phenomena in a correct way. Without science the mysteries of nature and society cannot reveal themselves to man and without reason and scientific method no social change can occur and the working classes cannot be liberated from the clutches of the ruling capitalists, from illiteracy, obscurantism, disease and darkness.

The eternal conflict between goodness and evil, true and false, will continue in various social forms, colours and hues according to the social conditions of a given epoch. The pre-capitalist societies saw this struggle between goodness and evil with reference to religion and its related categories of thought, vision, perception and emotion.

In the modern revolutionary times this conflict or contradiction is seen with reference to science and its related categories of thought, perception and emotion. Class struggle is now a scientific proposition and not a religious notion. In the pre-capitalist societies religion had to metaphorically simplify this conflict as a struggle between pharaohs (god-kings) and divinely-inspired prophets, between Demons and Men of God. The latter were guided by God and they believed that all life, truth, knowledge, wisdom, power and other bounties emanate from God, the Cause of all causes. Prophetic revolutions were guided by divine revelations. And divine guidance and truth helped liberate the oppressed human beings.

Modern social revolution is guided by science and modern revolutionaries are scholars and scientists who discover truth and liberate the working classes from the slavery of capitalists, both local and foreign. Truth is revealed to the revolutionaries as a sum-total of higher principles of social equality, brotherhood, love, justice, honesty and sincerity. The modern revolutionaries are the leaders and teachers of the modern proletariat. God still reveals truth—but through science and not through religion. Prophets will not come. Scientists, scholars and revolutionaries follow in their footsteps. In this sense, (modern) scholars, scientists, and revolutionaries who stand for truth, social equality, justice, honesty and courage, knowledge and wisdom, love and compassion for the suffering humanity, are the heirs of the prophets of yore.

INDEX

Abd Allah ibn Mas'ud, 201
Abu Sa'id al-Khudri, 228
Adam, the Prophet, 97, 101-103, 104-110.
'Ammar ibn Yasir, 201.
'Arab Peninsula, 3

Believers, 32, 43, 45, 61, 68, 206, 207-08.
Bilal, 201.
Binyamin (Benjamin), 150, 156.

Capitalism, 42, 211, 229, 231, 235, 248, 249.
    dependent, 231, 232.
    capitalist morality, 217, 230
Christianity, 237.
Class struggle, 1,2, 173, 192-3, 235, 237, 247, 249, 252, 255.

Da'ud, the prophet, 99.
Din ('way of life), 27, 203, 212-15

Equality, 48, 55-6, 66, 69, 199-200, 205, 208, 214.

Falsehood, 71-72
Feudalism, 210, 223-24, 231 249.
Feudal Islam, 211, 223
Feudal Morality, 210.
Fiqh (Jurisprudence), 236.
Freedom, 166

God, 35, 241-5.
God and man, 245.

Habil (Abel), 109.
Hajira (Hagar), 144
Haman, 31, 80.
Haram, the Sanctuary, 193.
Harun (Aaron), the prophet, 168, 172
Herod, 178
Hijra, Migration, 60, 231
    Muhajir, 60, 61, 64.
Hud, the prophet, 47, 99, 119

Ibrahim (Abraham), the prophet, 38, 47, 63, 99, 133-49, 197, 206
Idris, the prophet, 177
Inequality, 128, 211
'Isa (Jesus Christ), the Prophet, 24, 47, 99, 174-5, 177-84, 185-88, 191.
Ishaq (Isaac), the prophet, 144, 150
Islam, 34, 38.
    Arkan (pillars), of, 212
    Feudalist/capitalist conceptions of, 208
    Quranic concept of, 203-4
Isma'il, the prophet, 38, 144-8, 177, 209
Israelites, 167, 172-3, 177, 187, 226-7 and Zakat, 227
Isra'il, 187.

Jews, 176-7
Jihad, 31, 53-59, 199, 203. 209, 210, 231
Justice, 66-8

economic–, 161-2

Ka'ba, 38, 145, 193
Kafir, 40, 99, 203-04.

Liberation theology, 234-7, 240-41, 247-8
Lut (Lot), the prophet, 63, 144

Maryam (Mary), 174, 175, 178.
Mecca, 145, 193-5, 199
Medina (Yathrib), 48, 199.
Messiah (Masih), 174, 186-7
Morality, capitalist, 217, 230.
–feudalist, 217, 223-4, 227, 230.
– revolutionary, 226, 230.
Muhammad, the prophet, 8, 16, 17, 19, 24, 38-9, 47, 63, 99, 189-216, 225, 241
Musa (Moses), the prophet, 24, 30, 47, 63, 80-1, 167-173, 177, 191, 226.
Mushrik, 34-5, 38.
Muslim, 38, 203-5
Quranic definition of, 206-8
Mustad'afun, 46, 49, 55, 173, 197.
Mustakbarun, 46
Muzara'a, 42

New Testament (Evangel, Gospel), 178
Nuh (Noah), the prophet, 45, 47, 49, 50, 99, 111-118

Pakistan, 249.
Parables, 76-86
Pharaoh (Fir'awn), 30, 80, 167-173, 177, 240.
Pharisees, 179-84
Proletariat, 44-48, 51-52
Prophecy, 30, 234-5
Prophet-revolutionaries, 2-5, 17, 20-7, 33-40, 43-4, 47-9, 50, 64, 72, 95-9, 238. Social mission of, 30-31 and *Zakat,* 226-7, 234.

Qabil (Cain), 109
Quran, 80
Qura Zalima, 25, 73, 80, 193
Qur'an, 5, 8, 17, 19, 100, 241

Religion, 22-3, 235, 238, 241-2, 244, 247-9, 251-4
Religious ideology, 240.
Revelation, 8, 10, 11-14, 16-9, 23, 26-7, 28-30, 50
Revolution, 13, 15, 16, 23, 235, 249
Riba, 41
Righteous deeds, 209, 225

Sadaqa, 225-6, 228
Salat, 173, 176-7, 199, 204, 207-10, 220-3
the concept of, 218-9
Salih, the prophet, 99, 125
Salman, 201
Sarah, 144
Science, 23-4, 235, 243, 248, 252-5
Scientific method, 255
Scribes, 180
Shari'a, 232
Shirk, 34-6
Shu'ayb, 166, 201
Slavery, 166, 201
Social order, 22
Just, 22
Unjust, 25
of expoitation, 171
Socialism, 212, 235
Suhayb, 201

Tabuk, 65
Ta'if, 195
Torah (the Law), 189
Truth, 38, 71-79, 82, 86-90, 91-93

'Ulama' (religious scholars), 236
'Umar ibn 'Abd al-'Aziz, 228
Unbelievers (*Kafirun*), 68, 203

Wilayat al-faqih ('rule of the Jurisconsult'), 236

Yahya (John), the prophet, 178.
Ya'qub (Jacob), the prophet, 150-151, 156-8, 206
Yusuf (Joseph), the prophet, 99, 150-158

Zakat, 173, 176-7, 199-200, 204-205, 209, 210, 214, 220, 221, 228.
  Capitalist concept of, 229, 230.
  concept of, 218, 224
  feudalist concept of, 227, 229.
  function of, 225-6
  revolutionary concept of, 229.
Zayd ibn Haritha, 201
Zulm, 40-3, 173